# SPANISH GLASS

# FABER MONOGRAPHS ON GLASS
edited by R. J. Charleston

★

NINETEENTH CENTURY BRITISH GLASS
*Hugh Wakefield*

MODERN GLASS
*Ada Polak*

SPANISH GLASS
*Alice Wilson Frothingham*

(*in preparation*)
ROMAN GLASS
*D. B. Harden*

EIGHTEENTH CENTURY ENGLISH GLASS
*R. J. Charleston*

BOHEMIAN GLASS
*Karel Hetteš*

VENETIAN GLASS
*Paul Perrot*

ISLAMIC GLASS
*Ralph Pinder-Wilson*

A. *Vase, with enamelled and cold-gilt decorations.*
*Barcelona, about 1580. Ht. 9¼ in. (23.5 cm.)*
*The Hispanic Society of America, New York*
*(See pages 37–38)*

# SPANISH GLASS

by

ALICE WILSON FROTHINGHAM

*Curator of Ceramics*
*The Hispanic Society of America*

NEW YORK
THOMAS YOSELOFF

*First American Edition 1964*
*Published by Thomas Yoseloff Inc.*
*New York*

# CONTENTS

FOREWORD                                                    *page* 7

ACKNOWLEDGEMENTS                                                  9

INTRODUCTION                                                     11

1 MEDIEVAL SPANISH GLASS: ROMANESQUE AND GOTHIC
    PERIODS                                  19

2 CATALUÑA AND NEIGHBOURING REGIONS                             30

3 SOUTHERN SPAIN: ALMERÍA, GRANADA, SEVILLA                     52

4 CASTILLA: CADALSO, RECUENCO, NUEVO BAZTÁN AND
    OTHER GLASS CENTRES OF THE REGION        60

5 THE ROYAL FACTORY OF LA GRANJA DE SAN ILDEFONSO              72

MAP OF GLASS CENTRES IN SPAIN                                 88-9

BIBLIOGRAPHY                                                    90

INDEX                                                           93

5

# ILLUSTRATIONS

## COLOUR PLATES

A. Enamelled glass vase. Barcelona, about 1580   *frontispiece*

B. Flask. María, province of Almería, late sixteenth
century                                            *facing page* 34

C. Càntir. Cataluña, eighteenth century                     62

D. Covered jar. La Granja de San Ildefonso,
about 1775–85                                           84

## MONOCHROME PLATES
*at end of the book*

1–3. Medieval glass

4–45. Catalan glass

46–64. Glass of southern Spain

65–75. Glass of Castilla

76–96. Glass from the Royal Factory of La Granja de San Ildefonso

# FOREWORD

Where glass is concerned, as in other matters, Spain has been on the periphery of Europe. She has reacted to the various great movements within European glass-making, and not initiated them. Despite her dominant political position in the sixteenth century, she nevertheless became at that time a province of Venetian glass-making, although for a moment in the second half of the fifteenth century it seemed as if the Catalan glassmakers might lead the world. In the eighteenth century the *façon de Venise* was succeeded as the European mode by the Bohemian style of solid water-clear glass decorated by wheel-engraving, and this fashion was taken up at the Spanish Royal factory of La Granja de San Ildefonso, only to be replaced there towards the end of the century by the English style of massive cut crystal glass.

Despite this receptiveness to foreign influences, Spain took her captors captive. Spanish glass remains unmistakably Spanish. The source of this resilience is probably to be traced in the Southern provinces, where from the days of Moorish rule glass had been made in the great Islamic tradition, subtly transmuted as all Hispano-Moresque art was transmuted. This particular feeling for forms and ornaments permeates the Venetian-inspired glasses of the sixteenth and seventeenth centuries, and is discernible in La Granja glasses of the eighteenth century, although it blends perhaps less happily with these.

This continuity and marked personality of Spanish glass make it among the most interesting and attractive manifestations of the art to be found anywhere. Nobody is better qualified to anatomize it than Alice Wilson Frothingham, Curator of Ceramics at The Hispanic Society of America, New York. Herself guardian of an important collection of Spanish glass, and an expert in the kindred arts of pottery and porcelain, Mrs Frothingham through years of work in the collections of the Hispanic Society has had unique opportunities of steeping herself in the atmosphere of Spanish art. This highly developed feeling for things Spanish is matched by her knowledge of the Spanish sources and her thorough exploitation of them.

R. J. CHARLESTON

7

# ACKNOWLEDGEMENTS

Through the kindness of museum directors and curators in many countries, the author has received photographs and permission to illustrate objects from the collections under their care. The names of these museums and institutes are mentioned in captions under the illustrations. Private collectors, also, in Spain and in the United States, including the Countess of El Valle de Canet, Juan Prats, Miguel Mateu and Jerome Strauss, have been most gracious in granting similar privileges. Especial recognition should be given to the administrators of the Patrimonio Nacional for photographs of glass in the Royal Palace, Madrid, and for permission to reproduce them. Acknowledgement is made to the President and Trustees of The Hispanic Society of America for making available the resources of an extensive file of photographs belonging to the Society.

It may be said that Spanish glass has been collected in past centuries from the time when quantities of it left the glasshouses and entered the homes of its original owners. However, modern collecting of this glass began about a century ago and still continues. The Spaniards themselves were the first and principal collectors, and the results of their efforts, bequeathed and donated to museums, may be seen today in Madrid, Barcelona and other cities. The Museo Arqueológico Nacional in Madrid exhibits glasses from the Rico y Sinobas, Boix and Pérez Bueno collections. The Artíñano collection is now on view at the Museo de Artes Decorativas in the same city. Barcelona is fortunate in having the Cabot and Plandiura collections for its Museos de Arte. Also in this city, the Instituto Amatller de Arte Hispánico now has the glasses that belonged to the late Antonio Amatller. Through the generosity of Juan Prats, the institute's collection was increased in 1962 by the addition of his many pieces of Spanish glass. This union of the two collections brings together an extraordinary display of Roman, Catalan and Spanish glasses. At Peralada the Mateu collection has been installed in a special museum where it may be seen by scholar and student.

9

## Acknowledgements

Probably the largest collection of Spanish glass outside Spain is that in the Victoria and Albert Museum, although the British Museum and the Glasgow Museum own many pieces, and the Musée Curtius at Liège now has the Armand Baar collection, which contains numerous Spanish glasses. The Museum of Industrial Art at Prague owns a remarkable collection of Catalan and other Spanish glass, and the Hermitage Museum at Leningrad has about one hundred and fifty pieces, many of them Andalusian.

Colour transparencies and photographs of Spanish glasses in the museum of the Hispanic Society were made by Della K. Catuna, Margaret E. Jackson and Ann L. Siebert, members of the photographic staff. The map of glass centres was made by Frances Spalding, Curator of Records at the Hispanic Society.

Acknowledgement for reproduction privileges is given to the following photographers: Archives Photographiques d'Art et d'Histoire, Paris, plates 6, 8, 23A; Archivo de Arqueología Catalana (A. D. A. C.), Barcelona, plates 9A, 15B, 25B, 38A, 45B, 85A–B; Arthur Churchill, Ltd., London, plate 72; Photo. Corning Museum (for the Strauss collection), plates 28, 29, 33B, 51A, 64B, 84A; Cav. P. Fiorentini, Venice, plate 60; Gudiol, Barcelona, plates 7B, 21, 25A, 38B, 48B, 64C, 65B; Mas, Barcelona, plates 1, 2A–B, 7A, 11A–B, 12–15A, 16–20, 22, 23B, 24, 26, 27, 39A, 40, 43, 44, 66–70; Piaget, Saint Louis, plate 91; J. Ruiz Vernacci, Madrid, plates 36A–B, 57B, 94; Francisco Serra, Barcelona, plate 42.

# INTRODUCTION

Glass has been made in the Iberian Peninsula since the first years of the Christian era, when Hispania was under Roman domination. These conquerors imported glass objects in quantities from their eastern provinces of Syria and Egypt, and later from Gaul and the Rhineland. They may also have encouraged the wanderings of glass-blowers from the East or North Africa, like the Carthaginian 'opifex artis vitriae' who established himself in Gaul. Instructed by such itinerant masters, the Spaniards learned the technique of blowing a gather of viscous 'metal' on the end of a hollow pipe and so forming free-blown or mould-blown glasses. These men worked with mixtures coloured by minerals or compounds found in the natural state, but about the first century A.D. they knew how to make an almost colourless glass. By adding oxides of cobalt, manganese and antimony they produced deep sapphire, amethyst and topaz. They learned how to decorate cups and bowls with simple wheel-engraved lines by the third century, and over the next two hundred years they produced quantities of tableware, drinking vessels, bottles for perfumes and ointments, large cinerary urns and other articles for grave furnishings.

Hispano-Roman glass was composed, for the most part, of the ingredients included in all batches of glass – silica from sand and alkali for a flux to help the melting process. The silica usually contained iron impurities that turned the glass pale green, a defect which could be minimized by adding an oxide of manganese to the 'metal'. The glassmen of Spain, as in other Mediterranean countries, derived their alkali from plants growing in salt marshes, so that from the ashes of Salsola, Salicornia and other marine plants was extracted a carbonate of soda. This lixiviated soda ash containing a small amount of lime has been known for centuries as 'barilla', the main ingredient for soda-lime glass. As time progressed, Spanish barilla was to gain a great reputation for its excellent quality and to be exported to countries all over Europe.

Venice imported cargoes of barilla from Alicante for the Murano glass-houses, while sixteenth- and seventeenth-century glass-blowers working after the manner of the Venetians in Flanders, England and France recognized its superiority over other kinds. About 1570, when Cosimo I de'Medici was negotiating with a Muranese glass-blower to set up a furnace for manufacturing Venetian-type crystals at Florence, he promised the craftsman, as partial inducement for leaving Venice, that a ship would be sent to fetch this alkali from Spain.[1]

James Howell in 1621 wrote a letter describing how Alicantine barilla was made:

'I am now . . . come to **Alicant**[e], the chief Rendezvous I aimed at in **Spain,** for I am to send hence a Commodity called **Barrillia,** to Sir **Robert Mansel**[l], for making of Crystal Glass. . . . This **Barrillia** is a strange kind of Vegetable, and it grows no where upon the Surface of the Earth in that Perfection, as here: . . . It grows thus, It is a round thick earthy Shrub that bears Berries like Barberries, betwixt blue and green; it lies close to the Ground, and when it is ripe they dig it up by the Roots, and put it together in Cocks, where they leave it to dry many Days like Hay; then they make a Pit of a Fathom deep in the Earth, and with an Instrument like one of our Prongs, they take the Tuffs and put fire to them, and when the Flame comes to the Berries, they melt and dissolve into an **Azure** Liquor, and fall down into the Pit till it be full; then they dam it up, and some Days after they open it and find this **Barrillia** Juice turned to a blue Stone, so hard, that it is scarce malleable; it is sold at one hundred Crowns a Tun. . . .'[2]

So primitive was this method of preparation that we can easily believe it a survival from the Roman period.

An industry so well established among the Hispano-Romans as the manufacture of glass did not die out completely with the arrival of Visigothic tribes in the fifth century. For three hundred years Spain remained under their domination, an era when glassmaking existed, although at low ebb. Saint Isidore, bishop of Sevilla, whose death occurred in 636, wrote an entire chapter on the manufacture of glass as carried on in Spain, Italy and Gaul, commenting on ingredients for the pot-metal, on the general method for melting and blowing glass, the usual colours, the materials and processes necessary to make glass that was clear and colourless as crystal.[3]

Rare indeed are the glasses that have been attributed to the Visigoths, none of the objects differing radically in style from the Roman. There is less variety in shapes and in decoration, which is restricted principally to trailed threading and applied cabochons of glass. One of the most important

[1] G. Escolano, *Decada primera de la historia de la . . . ciudad y reyno de Valencia,* Valencia, 1610, vol. I, book 4, col. 665–6; G. Taddei, *L'Arte del vetro in Firenze e nel suo dominio,* Florence, 1954, pp. 48–9; app. XXVIII, pp. 115–16.

[2] James Howell, *Epistolae Ho-Elianae: familiar Letters Domestic and Foreign . . . ,* London, 11th edition, 1754, pp. 50–1 (letter dated 27 March, 1621).

[3] Saint Isidore, Bishop of Sevilla, *Etimologías. Versión castellana . . . ,* Madrid, 1951, book 16, chap. 16, pp. 401–2 (Biblioteca de autores cristianos).

pieces said to have been made in the Visigothic period is a rectangular paten of dark blue glass (Macaya collection, Barcelona) moulded with a fish in bas-relief. Another use for glass among the Visigoths was in their *cloisonné* jewellery, wherein false gems of blue, yellow, purple and green glass were set next to precious stones.

The ensuing invaders of the Peninsula were armies of Muslims from North Africa and the Near East – Syrians, Arabs, Berbers and Moors. From A.D. 711 until the tenth century, southern Spain was a wide-spread battlefield, where little encouragement for peaceful arts could have been found. The reign of the Umayyad Abd al-Rahman III brought order to the troubled Caliphate of Córdoba, and for a century this city equalled Baghdad in splendour. In luxurious palaces and a mosque built with the aid of foreign artists, the western caliphs lived among treasures brought from the East – sculptured columns and mosaics from Byzantium, gold-lustred pottery from Persia, velvets and gold-threaded silks from Mesopotamia. Excavations among the ruins of the Cordovan Caliph's palace at Medina az-Zahra revealed bowls of cut glass and fragments of mould-blown bottles that must surely have journeyed from Persia, Mesopotamia or Egypt, so closely do they resemble the artistic work of the East. There is, however, good reason to believe that Andalucía had native glass-blowers at work throughout the eleventh and twelfth centuries.

The first mention of them comes to us in the comments of Ibn Sa'id, a writer of Granada. He spoke of Almería and Málaga as famous for the manufacture of glass and specified that at Murcia the glass-blowers made large vases of the most exquisite and elegant shapes.[1] His remarks, written about 1274, imply that these cities had been glass-producing centres for a long time, perhaps for centuries. Another indication of such activity is the treatise, called in Spanish, *El lapidario*.[2] As the title implies, it deals primarily with the art of the lapidary, but it also contains formulae for glass mixtures and an explanation of the processes of blowing and annealing glass and decorating it with engraving, gilding and enamelling, as well as the methods for making lenses. Originally written in oriental Hebrew of the fifth or sixth century, this work was later translated into Arabic by an Hispano-Muslim named Abolais, whom one suspects of having supplied notes from some other source, such as the treatise by the German monk Theophilus. In 1248, Alfonso X of Castilla and León ordered the Arabic

[1] Ibn Sa'id as quoted by the seventeenth-century traveller and historian, Al-Makkari, in his *The History of the Mohammedan Dynasties in Spain . . . tr . . . by Pascual de Gayangos*, London, 1840, vol. I, pp. 51, 93.

[2] MS in the Escorial Library; M. Rico y Sinobas, *Del vidrio y sus artífices en España*, Madrid, 1873, pp. 6–10.

version to be translated into Castillian, and again the translator added supplementary comments.

It seems entirely probable that the glass blown by Hispano-Muslims in these early centuries started a long tradition that underwent little change until modern times. In the glass vessels of the eighteenth century we detect an influence of early Islamic forms and of the blowing technique and plastic ornamentation used in Roman glass centres of Syria or Palestine. This lag in development left southern Spain isolated and apathetic toward the fresh sources of inspiration that were offering new ideas to glassworkers in other regions.

The protection of Spanish industry was a particular concern of the monarchs, Ferdinand and Isabel (1479–1516), and with this in mind they forbade the importation of foreign goods. Their grandson, the Emperor Charles V (1516–56), holding an entirely diverse opinion, encouraged foreign imports and levied high taxes on Spanish manufacturers. The result to Castillian industries was disastrous, but firm action on the part of the Cortes of Aragón and Cataluña and resistance from the Catalan guilds rescued industry in that great region from the general financial depression. The succession of Charles to the Spanish throne united Spain and Flanders under his rule, and thus brought the two countries into close relationship. The alliance had its effect on the glass industry, undoubtedly fostering an interchange of glassworkers and encouraging the spread of Venetian-style glasses.

At Antwerp, the Venetians founded in 1541 the first furnace in the Spanish Netherlands for blowing glass 'à la façon de Venise'. There they worked under the patronage of the Emperor Charles and of his sister, María of Hungary, while she was governor of the Low Countries. Privileges granted by her for the establishment of a glass furnace were renewed in 1556, when her nephew Philip became king of Spain. This monarch awarded the same rights to Jacomo di Francesco, 'Venetian, master of the furnaces for making crystal glasses in our city of Antwerp'. Venetian-type crystals blown there and in other Flemish centres imitated the originals so well that even contemporary experts could not distinguish between them. During this and the following century, many Venetian-style glasses were exported from Flanders to Spain, where purchasers may have been under the impression that they were buying the products of Venice itself.[1]

Whether Spanish glassmen picked up any knowledge of their craft from written sources would have depended upon their ability to read. They had

[1] A. W. Frothingham, *Barcelona Glass in Venetian Style*, New York, 1956, pp. 18–19.

available to them Biringuccio's *De la pirotechnica*, describing how glass was made in 1540, probably in Venice since his book was published there, and Tommaso Garzoni's *La piazza universale*, Venice, 1585. A Spanish version of the latter, translated by Cristóbal Suárez de Figueroa and published at Madrid in 1615, omitted those parts of the original that would have been interesting only to Italians and substituted for them data pertaining to the Spaniards. About glass, the translator wrote, 'Moreover, when one particularly wishes to make glasses of opaque white ("blancos de esmalte"), calcined tin is added; this is called "latticinio", with which several types of work are done on crystal glasses.' The Spaniard went on to state what minerals must be added to the glass to give different colours – red, green, or emerald. 'These are the various colours from which are made threads to decorate the crystal glasses, forming also buttons, stones for rings, rosary beads, chains and a thousand other trinkets. At the present time in Murano [Venice] and Barcelona, so precise is this work that everything imaginable may be done with glass and crystal.'[1]

Probably the Catalan priest, Pere Gil, had no intention of teaching prospective glass-blowers when, in the late sixteenth century, he wrote a description of the processes of manufacture and the composition of glass 'metals'. If his *Historia natural de Catalunya* had ever been published, it would have explained something of the mysteries of glassmaking to the average reader. He distinguished between three kinds of glass, the first being a coarse variety of 'pedra albanesa', probably a kind of quartz, mixed with soda ash from a herb picked at Tortosa and on the Llobregat plain. A much better, clearer glass was that containing barilla from Valencia. The glass made with this soda-lime ash contained also the 'pedra albanesa' and a small amount of the mineral called 'sanguinea' (manganese dioxide?). The latter ingredient served to clarify the glass and correct a greenish tint. The best glass of all included ashes of tartar, the sediment found in wine-skins. This substance mixed with two kinds of pulverized quartz ('pedra albanesa' and 'cristall cru') was placed in the furnace and to it was added a little manganese from Genoa. This mixture produced 'crystal' glass of the clearest, purest and 'most perfect' kind. To colour glass, various chemicals in the natural state were added to the pot: tin and lead oxides for opaque white; zaffre, a mineral containing cobalt for blue; and for red, the filings from copper kettles.[2]

[1] T. Garzoni, [*La piazza universale*, Sp. tr. with additions by Cristóbal Suárez de Figueroa] *Plaza universal*, Perpiñan, 1630 (1629), *f* 262, *tr.*
[2] Pere Gil, *Historia natural de Catalunya*, *f* 36, quoted in J. M. Gudiol Ricart, *Els vidres catalans*, Barcelona [1936], pp. 154–7. The manuscript belongs to the Biblioteca del Seminario, Barcelona.

## Introduction

The account of glassmaking which exerted the most influence on Spanish glassworkers was Antonio Neri's *L'Arte vetraria*, first published at Florence in 1612. His treatise, based on experiences in an Antwerp glass factory run by Venetians, was translated into several languages and published during the seventeenth and eighteenth centuries, each time with commentaries. In Castilla, a translation done by a master glassman in 1676 never left the manuscript state, but a later version with copious additional material, published in 1780, became a handbook for Spanish artisans.[1]

Glass factories flourished where essential materials were abundant. Sand, barilla, refractory clays for furnaces and crucibles, abundant firewood and proximity to routes of transportation, all those necessities determined the locality where the glass-blower chose to establish himself. Certain regions of Spain more favourable than others encouraged the industry, and thus, in Cataluña particularly, the manufacture of glass began at an early date and flourished for centuries. What tools these workmen used we learn from an inventory of equipment belonging to a furnace at Vallbona in 1664. Irons included pontils, blowpipes, tongs, pincers, shovels and sledge-hammers to break up the barilla. At the entrance to the furnace were fifty-three quintals of soda ash, baskets of all sorts for carrying loads of glass to market and a goatskin sieve for sifting the powdered ingredients of glass mixtures.[2]

From the thirteenth to the sixteenth century, artists worked throughout Spain at designing and composing stained-glass windows for Gothic cathedrals and churches. To execute the commissions of prelate and prince, these men came southward from Flanders, Germany and France. Later on, local artists joined the foreigners. Within or near the building for which windows were to be made, these men would set up furnaces and work-rooms, devoting themselves exclusively to a single task until it was done. Then on to another assignment they went, travelling from city to city. The coloured glasses for windows were cut from either crown glass or muff glass, both types having been made with a blowpipe. For crown glass the soft bulb or paraison was collapsed on the end of an iron rod, called a pontil, by spinning it rapidly to form a disc. In making muff glass the blower worked the bulb out to an elongated shape, cut off the ends and then split the cylinder lengthways. After reheating the cylinder he flattened the glass into a sheet. The production of stained-glass windows will not be considered in this book. Neither will glass gems be discussed, since they relate more nearly to the jeweller's art than to glassmaking.

[1] M. G. Suárez y Núñez, *Memorias instructivas, y curiosas*, Madrid, 1780, vol. 4, pp. 185–468 (Memorias L–LII : *Sobre el vidrio, y los esmaltes*).
[2] Gudiol Ricart, *op. cit.*, pp. 160–1.

## Introduction

Among the special skills associated with the industry was the ability to turn out glass made at the lamp. The process described by Father Gil was the same in the sixteenth century as at present. The workman supplied himself with glass tubes and rods, a few small tools and an oil lamp. Picking up a tube, he then placed one end in the flame until it became red hot, and with the cool end of the tube in his mouth, he blew a small bubble. By heating a rod and spinning it to a fine thread, by twisting, bending, welding and pinching he could shape all sorts of miniature objects. Tiny animals and insects, minuscule cages holding birds, little plates of fruit, replicas of household vessels and furniture, flower gardens in minute scale, in fact, anything that his imagination dictated the artisan could make with the lamp's aid.

Clear glass flattened into sheets for window-panes and mirrors was a branch of manufacture which had a slow start in Spain, developing most fully in the eighteenth century. To make sheet glass, the colourless 'metal' called 'crystal' was blown into the form of a muff, which, when opened up and flattened into sheets, could be cut into panes of limited size. They were sold also to mirrormakers who quicksilvered the backs and polished the front surfaces. Window-panes, considered a great luxury, were purchased sparingly even by the king and his wealthiest subjects. In most houses, wooden shutters and iron grilles protected the inhabitants from cold winds, rains and the entry of thieves. Even in the early nineteenth century, travellers to Spain commented on the lack of glazing in the windows. Mansions in Madrid and royal palaces everywhere in the country must be considered exceptions, for they were well supplied with window-panes and wall-mirrors once the Royal Glass Factory became established in 1728 at the palace of La Granja de San Ildefonso.

Later chapters of this book will deal with the expansion of the glass industry in the different regions of Spain, as it was affected in turn by 'Damascus' enamelled glass, Venetian glass and, finally, the crystal glass of Germany and England. It should not be assumed, however, that Spaniards entirely followed the ideas of others, for these masters made their own contributions to the craft. Their creativeness shows forth especially in the glasses produced in Cataluña and again in the work of eighteenth-century Castilla.

# I

## MEDIEVAL SPANISH GLASS: ROMANESQUE AND GOTHIC PERIODS

From early times Cataluña was a crossroads where goods and treasures arrived by sea from the ports of Italy and the East or overland from France. By the mid-thirteenth century Cataluña, including the Balearic Islands, was a principality of the Crown of Aragón, a kingdom which also embraced Valencia. Cataluña's boundaries to the north enclosed the Roussillon and Cerdagne, territory that ultimately became part of France. This north-eastern principality, open to foreign influences, progressed early and competently in developing its own skills.

We know that Catalan glassworkers of the eleventh and twelfth centuries blew wine cups and globular flasks with long necks for the dinner table. None of these objects has survived, but representations of them appear in scenes of feasting that illustrate the eleventh-century Bible of Ripoll in the Vatican Library, and that of Roda in the Bibliothèque Nationale, Paris, and the twelfth-century Homilies of Breda in the Museo Diocesano, Gerona. A twelfth-century mural from the Church of Santa María at Mur, now in the Boston Museum of Fine Arts, shows the lamps shaped like cups which customarily hung in Romanesque sanctuaries.

Bishops, consecrating new churches in country parishes of Cataluña, sealed holy relics within the altars as part of the ceremony. The dignitary who performed this office in 1086 at the Monastery of San Esteban, Bañolas, first placed a piece of the true Cross into a 'crystal' casket before enclosing it in the high altar.[1] This crystal may, or may not, have been rock-crystal. Several glass reliquaries, green or brownish in tone, have been found in remote churches and monastery chapels throughout the region.

---

[1] J. Villanueva, *Viage literario a las iglesias de España*, Madrid, 1850, vol. 14, p. 320.

At least six are spherical or pear-shaped bottles, their long necks broken off and closed with sealing-wax bearing the stamp of the episcopal ring. Known as lipsanothecas, these bottles are like eleventh-century Islamic glasses, their mould-blown forms rippled by lozenge, honeycomb and 'pigeon-eye' patterns. Although a Catalan source has been claimed for them,[1] they might better be considered rare treasures from the East.

The Monastery of Poblet, near Tarragona, is perhaps the earliest documented site in Cataluña for glassmaking. An agreement made by the abbot and the prior with a glass-blower named Guillem is dated the nineteenth day of August, 1189. The monastery granted Guillem the privilege of gathering the 'herbs necessary to his trade', probably glasswort, for which he was to pay a tithe and supply the monks with two hundred pounds of sheet glass each Eastertide. For an additional four hundredweights of glass the community would give Guillem his food, and two hundred pounds more would assure him of a proper funeral. The exact site of the glassworks was near the monastery, at a spring called Narola. From this location in 1935 were excavated quantities of glass fragments, which give further evidence that the site was occupied formerly by a glass furnace.[2]

The archives of Barcelona trace the record of glassmaking in that city back to the early fourteenth century, although the guild of glassworkers undoubtedly had a far earlier origin.[3] An edict of 1324 pronounced glass furnaces a fire hazard and prohibited their construction within the city boundaries. Later this ordinance was put aside by royal command, and glassworkers again established their furnaces inside the walls. About this time two streets, the 'Calle de los Vidrieros' and the 'Calle de la Vidriería', acquired the names that designate them as the glass-blowers' and the glass merchants' quarters.[4]

The journey of a Barcelonese glass-blower, Guillem Barceló, to Mallorca in 1347 proved eventful for him. In direct opposition to an old ordinance prohibiting glass furnaces within the city limits, he sought and obtained royal permission to build one at Palma. The king granted his request because Guillem's new-style furnace consumed less wood than former

[1] Gudiol Ricart, *op. cit.*, pp. 68–9; plates 1–3.
[2] E. Toda i Güell, *La collecció de vidres antics de Poblet* (in Societat Arqueológica Tarraconense, Tarragona, *Butlletí arqueològic*, April-June 1935, pp. 46–9).
[3] Most of the information on medieval glassmaking in Cataluña is the result of research by Monsignor José Gudiol y Cunill in the archives of Barcelona, Vich, Mallorca and elsewhere. Some of his findings were published during his lifetime, but it was the monumental book, *Els vidres catalans*, by his nephew José Gudiol Ricart, published in 1936, which made available the major part of these archival studies.
[4] A. de Capmany y de Montpalau, *Memorias históricas sobre la marina, comercio y artes de la antigua ciudad de Barcelona*, Madrid, 1779, vol. 1, pt. 3, pp. 135, 18; Gudiol Ricart, *op. cit.*, p. 32.

types. Furthermore, he promised to import this fuel from the mainland in order not to deplete the island forests. The city council, resentful perhaps that the king had overruled them or fearful still that a glass furnace might set their city afire, resisted Guillem with every possible evasion.[1] The significance of his venture to the history of Mallorcan glassmaking lies in the fact that his petition refers to an ordinance ancient even in 1347.

Another glassmaker, Nicholau Coloma, was more kindly treated by a later council. His request for the exclusive right of making and selling glass at Palma was granted in 1398 and proclaimed through the streets by the town crier. Prospective customers were informed that Nicholau would sell flasks, goblets and bottles of all shapes at bargain prices, provided that they were bought for personal use and not resold or exported from the island.[2]

The glass industry in the Roussillon during the thirteenth and fourteenth centuries centred around Perpignan, Collioure, Elne and Palau. The first member of a notable family of glassworkers was recorded in 1334 at Palau, Berenguer Xatart. Succeeding generations of men by that name built up the town's great reputation for glass to the point where it became known as Palau-del-Vidre. The Countess of Artois in 1316 alluded in her inventory to the glasses of southern France, which the Count had purchased toward the end of the previous century.[3]

The appearance of medieval Catalan glass is conveyed to us not only through annotations in inventories, but also through representations painted on wooden panels by the fourteenth-century artists Ferrer Bassa, Jaume and Pere Serra and their school, Lluis Borrassà and his followers. In illustrating the Last Supper or Herod's feast, these men depicted tables set with serving dishes for meats and fruits, goblets, bottle-necked decanters and wine jugs. The inventories add considerably to the number of shapes by recording 'ampolles', or two-handled containers for floral waters and oils, 'barrals' or casks for storing wine, often covered with woven straw or palm. Glass lanterns, lamps and candelabra are mentioned, as well as special glasses used by the doctor and the apothecary. 'Canadelles', or ecclesiastical cruets, are noted in an account book of purchases made in 1395–96 for the cathedral at Palma de Mallorca,[4] and many other shapes could be mentioned.

[1] E. K. Aguiló, *Industrias mallorquinas: Fábricas de cinabrio y de vidrio* [*1347*] (in Sociedad Arqueológica Luliana, Palma, *Boletín,* November 1890, año 6, pp. 318–20).
[2] Aguiló, *Documento sobre la fabricación de vidrio en Mallorca* [*1398*] (in Sociedad Arqueológica Luliana, Palma, *Boletín,* 10 June, 1889, año 5, p. 88).
[3] P. Vidal, *Guide historique et pittoresque dans le département des Pyrénées-Orientales,* Perpignan, 1879, p. 184; J. Barrelet, *La verrerie en France de l'époque gallo-romaine à nos jours,* Paris, 1953, p. 38.
[4] Frothingham, *Hispanic Glass,* New York, 1941, pp. 10, 172–3, notes 22–3.

## Medieval Spanish Glass: Romanesque and Gothic Periods

Despite the flourishing condition of native glass-blowing centres, there was much importation of foreign glass to Cataluña. Barcelona's vast fleet of ships brought the Kingdom of Aragón into direct contact with every Mediterranean port and even sailed into the dread Atlantic to seek the harbours of Flanders. Catalan sea captains trafficking in the eastern Mediterranean brought back rare glasses from Alexandria, Beirut and Damascus. These merchants knew how greatly their patrons prized the fragile and exotic glasses of the Near East, which they carefully saved and handed down as heirlooms. The young son of a Catalan apothecary at Cervera (Lérida province) inherited a decanter of 'Damascus' glass which brought a good price in 1373 when it was put up at auction.[1]

Besides being shipped as merchandise, glass was carried home by pilgrims and other travellers. Enamelled glass lamps from the Near East found their way into Christian churches of Spain, perhaps as thank offerings for a safe journey, and 'Damascus' glass held an honoured place among the possessions of king, noble and high official. King Martin I of Aragón (1395–1410) had a 'Damascus' glass dish elaborately mounted on a chased silver-gilt pedestal embellished with an enamelled and gilt eagle.[2] Evidently the words 'vidre de Damas' or 'vidre domesquí' meant to medieval Catalans the special type of enamelled glass that came from Syria, made either at Damascus or Aleppo, since they often omitted to mention in inventories of their personal goods whether or not it was enamelled. There are references to 'Damascus' glass, however, that leave no doubt as to its being so decorated. One document of the year 1396 records a rose-water sprinkler ('almorratxa') 'of blue glass decorated with the work of Damascus', and a few entries of the early fifteenth century are clearer still in their notations of 'Damascus' glasses that were 'painted', or 'painted in several colours'.[3] Pieces designated as having come from Alexandria were probably of Syrian manufacture, since Egypt was an outlet for much enamelled glass from Syria, then its political dependency. Beirut, a city mentioned in the inventory of a fifteenth-century Barcelonese sailor, was more probably a port for shipping glass than a centre of glassmaking.[4]

Fourteenth-century Catalan references to enamelled glasses do not state

---

[1] E. Moliné y Brasés, *Inventari y encant d'una especieria cerverina del segle XIV* (in R. Academia de Buenas Letras, Barcelona, *Boletín*, October–December 1911, año II, pp. 195–204).

[2] *Inventari dels bens mobles del rey Martí d'Aragó*, pub. by J. Massó Torrents (in *Revue hispanique*, Paris, 1905, vol. 12, p. 530).

[3] Frothingham, *Barcelona Glass*, pp. 2–3; note 5. Mr R. J. Charleston suggests that these glasses may have been cold painted rather than enamelled.

[4] J. Soler y Palet, *L'art a la casa al segle XV* (in R. Academia de Buenas Letras, Barcelona, *Boletín*, 1916, vol. 8, p. 388).

always that these objects originated in Damascus, thereby leaving the reader to speculate on the possibility of their having been domestic imitations. That Syrian glass was copied we know from an order given at Tortosa in the year 1387. The city council directed Domingo Valls, a painter, to buy a glass lamp either of Damascus manufacture or an imitation, 'obrada o contrafeta de Damasc', to be hung in the council chamber before a statue of Saint Christopher.[1] Excavations in future will probably turn up material furnishing additional proof that enamelled glass was produced in fourteenth-century Cataluña. Preliminary digging near San Feliú de Guixols brought to light a fourteenth-century glass furnace and fragments with enamelled designs that look both Arabic and Catalan in style.[2]

Besides being blown to form tableware, glass took on many other aspects at this time. It was shaped into beads for rosaries, necklaces and trimming for ladies' gowns. Glass stones instead of precious gems were encrusted on jewellery, silver or gold plate and statues of sculptured wood. Mirrors, some designated as shaving mirrors, were cut from glass panes, polished and framed.

An odd fashion made its way to Cataluña, probably from France, about the first quarter of the fourteenth century. Sheets of blue glass were fixed in arcadings behind bas-relief sculptures of alabaster. The custom lasted only until the end of the century, when sculptors returned to their former method of painting backgrounds. Two documents, dated 1354 and 1380, record the order of King Peter IV of Aragón for royal tombs to be installed at the Monastery of Poblet. These sarcophagi were to be carved with little figures of mourners set against blue glass backgrounds.[3]

As the fifteenth century began, the glass-blowers of Barcelona were becoming extremely important citizens, master craftsmen so clever that their work attracted extravagant praise. Making certain that the entire city saw their products, they followed a custom of long standing and held fairs yearly on the first of January. Every glasshouse displayed its finest and most beautiful pieces in stalls along the streets. The city councillors, riding in cavalcade, headed a crowd of people who came to admire the shining products of the blowpipe.

In 1455, the guild of glassworkers united with the weavers of esparto grass to form a new guild and brotherhood under the protection of Saint

[1] Gudiol Ricart, *op. cit.*, p. 37.
[2] Information obtained from letters written by Luis Llubiá Munné, from Barcelona, 16 December, 1956, and 18 January, 1961.
[3] A. Rubió y Lluch, *Documents per l'historia de la cultura catalana mig-eval*, Barcelona, 1921, vol. 2, pp. 103–4, 203–4; Barrelet, *op. cit.*, pp. 40–2.

Bernardino. An ordinance of the following year regulated their privileges and enumerated in detail their religious duties and charitable activities toward their fellow members. Permission had to be obtained from the guild if shopkeepers wished to sell glass within the city, and a tax was paid to its treasury for the favour. The growing strength of the guild had a significant effect on city government after Alfonso V decreed that one of their number might be represented on the Barcelona council. Accordingly, Pere Gallart was elected in 1455, the first glass-blower to sit on this board of five members. Later on, glass-blowers and esparto-weavers were required permanently to fill two places on the council.[1]

The edict against glass furnaces within the city of Barcelona drove glass-blowers to smaller communities in the province, not far distant from the capital. The Sala family ran their glassworks at Vallromanas from the time when Antoni established his furnace in 1417. Francesch had charge of the factory in 1461, probably the same Francesch Sala, 'glass-blower of Barcelona', whose few possessions were inventoried in 1485. Two years later, Vicenç was operating the Sala furnace at Vallromanas, but in 1489 he and his sons wandered to Moncada. There they established a glassworks, which they promised the Barcelona council would bring great honour and reputation to the town.[2] Perhaps their move was occasioned by the success of a glass factory installed there three years previously by Antoni Sadurní, citizen of Barcelona. Antoni, an embroiderer and one of a family celebrated for this art, had considered his venture in glass manufacture an opportunity to bring together a group of master craftsmen from distant places. One of Moncada's glassworkers, Pere Mata, left his shop in 1498, travelled northward to Vich and began operating a new furnace.[3]

Farther from Barcelona than Moncada, Mataró was probably as thriving a glass centre in the fifteenth century as it was in the seventeenth. A furnace at Granollers del Vallés was leased by its owner in 1491 to Jaume Savertés, who may have been a Gascon. Along with the furnace came a supply of glass metal in the crucible, all ready for use. The names of certain towns, such as Vallvidrera, five kilometers from Barcelona, and Vidreras, situated in the province of Gerona, indicate that glassmaking was the principal industry in these communities. Another site in Gerona, the castle of Cruilles, was the destination, in 1418, of the glass-blower Pere Xatart, member of the famous Palau-del-Vidre family. This northern section of

[1] Gudiol Ricart, *op. cit.*, pp. 38, 136–9, note 43; Capmany, *op. cit.*, pp. 134–5.
[2] Soler, *op. cit.*, p. 300.
[3] Gudiol Ricart, *op. cit.*, pp. 38–9.

Cataluña, the Roussillon, continued active in the manufacture of glass with furnaces busy at Perpignan, Vallbona, Villalonga and other towns.[1]

South of Barcelona, the province of Tarragona had its own glass centres. The provincial capital still has a street named 'Carrer del Vidre', indicating that glass was sold in its shops. In 1409, a company was formed between Jaume Roger, glass-blower from Tortosa, and Pere Salvat, a writer of Tarragona, who put up the capital for the scheme. Business prospered for three years; then, without balancing the accounts or dividing the profits with his partner, Jaume Roger fled to Flix, also in Tarragona province, where he started another glassworks.[2]

To the west of Tarragona, in the Aragonese province of Zaragoza, lies Caspe, a city recognized for the high quality of the glass which it produced so plentifully in the fifteenth century. Remains of furnaces found within its boundaries a few years ago and fragments of glass in eighteenth-century Catalan style are tangible proof that here was a great and long-lived centre.[3] Not much has been learned about the glass industry in Aragón except for these facts about Caspe.

Little more is known about glassmaking in Valencia, and yet there must have been a glass furnace in the capital city, since the street-name 'Forn del Vidre' (Glass Furnace), which survived until modern times, marked its location.[4] From the description of Valencian glasses in inventories we may surmise that they were of ordinary quality, principally for utilitarian purposes, as the gallon-sized pharmacy jars of green and colourless glass that a Cordovan apothecary purchased in 1502. A German traveller in 1494 mentioned the 'superb glasses' of Valencia and compared them favourably with those of Barcelona.[5]

Fifteenth-century reports of glass-blowers within the Valencian region give an idea of activity in scattered areas. Bernat Camporelles, a glassmaker of Murviedro is mentioned in 1418 and the acts of the town council at Elche record manufacture there. During August 1452, the council ordered buildings to be erected on a certain site, one house to contain a glass furnace. An artisan, Nadal Torres, leased the establishment on the understanding

[1] Gudiol Ricart, *op. cit.*, pp. 39–41, 140–1, note 54; Saint-Quirin, *Les verriers du Languedoc, 1290–1790* (in Société Languedocienne de Géographie, Montpellier, *Bulletin*, 1905, vol. 28, p. 384).
[2] S. Capdevila, *La industria vidriera a Tarragona* (in Societat Arqueológica Tarraconense, Tarragona, *Butlletí arqueològic*, April–June 1933, època 3, p. 243).
[3] L. Pérez Bueno, *Vidrios y vidrieras*, Barcelona, 1942, pp. 67–8.
[4] V. Boix, *Valencia histórica y topográfica*, Valencia, 1862, vol. l, p. 319.
[5] J. Gestoso y Pérez, *Ensayo de un diccionario de los artífices que florecieron en Sevilla*, Sevilla [1909] vol. 3, p. 456; J. Puyol, *Jerónimo Münzer. Viaje por España y Portugal en los años 1494 y 1495* (in R. Academia de la Historia, Madrid, *Boletín*, January 1924, vol. 84, p. 75).

that he might hold it as long as he filled the official position of town glass-blower. The councillors loaned him a sum of money to help finance the initial expenses of constructing his furnace, but later decided against buying the property originally indicated. They chose instead two sites on a street where, years previously, there had been a glass furnace. Thus, we learn that glassmaking at Elche was an industry established long before the mid-fifteenth century. Another glassman of Elche in 1453 carried a load of his products on muleback to Murcia, only to have them confiscated by the magistrate because he became involved in a street fight. Five years later the glass furnace at Elche again changed hands when the council leased it to another operator.[1]

Little can be said about the history of glassmaking during the fifteenth century in other regions of Spain. At present, documentary material is almost entirely lacking, but the isolated details which have turned up indicate that the craft was practised in Castilla and in Murcia, to the southeast. Burgos was the gathering place of Moorish and Jewish glass-blowers during the late years of the century. Evidently these workmen filled menial jobs and lived in segregated quarters of the city. In 1490, Pedro de Medina, a converted Jew, was so badly treated by the owner of a glass factory that he broke away and hired himself to Aluceynt, a Moorish glass-blower.[2] As a glass centre Cadalso de los Vidrios was probably the most prolific in Castilla, and with the advent of the next century, glass made at its furnaces was designated as comparable with that of Barcelona. At Guisando, in Avila province, two glass furnaces were operating from 1478 to 1480 or longer, both having paid rental to the Monastery of San Jerónimo for the use of its property. A remote origin for the glass industry in Murcia is implied in a traveller's account of 1494. After visiting Alhama, a town of this province, he described its traditional methods of making glass from sand and barilla.[3]

Toward the end of the century, the glass of Barcelona became famous not only locally but throughout the nation, and even in Italy. Contemporary writers were extravagant in their praise of it. Jerónimo Paulo, telling of the finest products of the Catalan city in 1491, wrote to Paolo Pamphili in Rome that Barcelona glass, much esteemed at the Roman court, rivalled that of Venice. The Sicilian traveller, Lucio Marineo, after journeying through

[1] Gudiol Ricart, *op. cit.*, p. 41; P. Ibarra y Ruiz, *Elche; materiales para su historia*, Cuenca, 1926, pp. 145-6.

[2] T. López Mata, *Morería y judería* (in R. Academia de la Historia, Madrid, *Boletín*, October-December 1951, vol. 129, p. 350).

[3] J. F. Riaño y Montero, *The Industrial Arts in Spain*, London, [2nd edition] 1890, p. 240; Puyol, *op. cit.*, pp. 74-5.

## Medieval Spanish Glass: Romanesque and Gothic Periods

Spain during the reign of Ferdinand and Isabel, said that the best glass in the entire country was made in Barcelona.[1]

Large quantities of glassware continued throughout the fifteenth century to be blown in Cataluña and on the island of Mallorca, some of whose workers learned the processes at Barcelona. Glasses were represented, principally in inventories of the period, as being blue, purple, tawny yellow and 'white', that is to say, uncoloured and transparent. Many were in variegated colours to imitate chalcedony, others were 'painted with divers colours'. The patterns were seldom described, although an entry for the year 1472 points to an Islamic type of decoration with the words, 'pintada a la morisca'.[2] Until mid-century the quantity of enamelled glass noted in inventories as from the Near East ranked about equally with the Catalan imitations, but gradually any mention of 'Damascus' glass disappeared from the records. By about 1450, domestic glass with enamelled decorations had replaced completely the type formerly imported from Syria.

Shapes mentioned in fifteenth-century inventories are mostly repetitions of those named in the previous century. Vases called 'pitxers' and 'pitxells' were for the purpose of holding flowers, while 'confiters' were covered jars for sweets, preserves or rose honey. Salt dishes mounted in silver or unusually shaped, like the Moor's-head salt listed in 1449, dominated the table setting.[3] To overcome abuses and excess charges imposed by the glass merchants of Palma de Mallorca, the city council in 1453 drew up a price list for the observance of all who sold glass. This list is of interest for the kinds of glass noted, as the shapes are identical with those common on the mainland. Certain vases were recorded as having been made from ordinary glass with a yellowish tint. Decanters of the greatest value were shaped 'like those of Barcelona', blown from transparent, colourless glass made with sand and barilla from the ashes of 'ciricorn', the local variety of prickly saltwort. High-stemmed goblets blown from metal of the same quality were equally valuable.[4]

Catalan glasses dating back to the Gothic period are of the utmost rarity. Aside from the numerous broken bits cast away by owners long ago or discarded as cullet by glassworkers near their furnaces, the few complete, or nearly complete, glasses might be listed briefly. Fragments, some of

[1] L. Marineo, *Obra . . . de las cosas memorables de España* [Alcalá de Henares] 1539, $v^{of}$ V.
[2] J. Gudiol y Cunill, *De vidrios esmaltados catalanes*, tr. from *De vidres esmaltats catalans* in *La Veu de Catalunya* (in L. Planell, *Vidrio*, Barcelona, 1948, vol. 2, p. 85).
[3] Gudiol Ricart, *op. cit.*, p. 43.
[4] *Tarifa impuesta a los vendedores de objetos de cristal* [*1453*] (in Sociedad Arqueológica Luliana, Palma, *Boletín*, 25 September, 1889, año 5, pp. 141–2).

which have been reconstructed as decanters, cruets, goblets, vases and bowls, have been found during excavations on the grounds and other property belonging to the Monasteries of Poblet and Santas Creus. From the Monastery of San Benet de Bages came two cruets of yellowish glass (Plate 1), with curved spouts and long necks encircled by glass threading. Excavations near two castles in the locality of Vich, at a convent in Villa-franca del Panadés and at several other sites have been equally productive. Although badly eroded, a goblet (Plate 2A) of uncoloured glass found in a sepulchre at Santas Creus displays a graceful, trumpet-shaped bowl resting on an annulated hollow knop and a conical foot. This piece has been placed chronologically in the fourteenth century, but a later dating seems prefer-able. Another goblet of yellowish glass (Macaya collection, Barcelona) also might better be ascribed to the late fifteenth century. Reconstructed from fragments found in the waster heap of an ancient pottery at Paterna (Valencia province), it has a mould-blown bowl fluted around the lower portion, which rests on a three-part knop and a ribbed, conical foot. Interesting to compare with these two goblets, and the one that follows, is a glass said to have been found in a Jewish cemetery in Damascus. Trailed cords pinched into a diamond-mesh ornament the bowl of this goblet which has been attributed to Venice of the fifteenth century.[1]

About this time, the glassworkers of Barcelona province began to produce enamelled glass that rivalled the Venetian in artistry. To these men and to this period we attribute a group of glasses that show the influence of Venice yet have a distinctly Spanish character.[2] Of their number is a goblet of transparent greyish glass (Plate 2B) shaped somewhat like the preceding two, except that the trumpet bowl rests directly on the conical base, giving a more solid look. Moulded ribbing pinched into a network of diamond-meshes on the bowl adds to the sturdiness. Around the rim runs a broad band of white chevrons and pearling in yellow, white and green. Flames of white enamel sparkle within the meshes, and rows of white pearling encircle the base. Though coarsely drawn, the chevron motif combines a Moresque zigzig and a trefoil common in Gothic tracery, to compose a Mudejar (or Hispano-Muslim) pattern.

Another goblet to be considered in the same category was blown in cobalt-blue glass (Plate 3) and enamelled predominantly in white, with touches of green, rose-red, and cold-painted gilt. Shaped like an inverted bell set upon a hollow, ribbed knop and a conical foot, it recalls the covered

[1] The glass is in The Ruth Bryan Strauss Memorial Foundation, no. S775. The Corning Museum of Glass, *Three Great Centuries of Venetian Glass*, Corning (N. Y.), 1958, pp. 27–8.
[2] Frothingham, *Barcelona Glass*, pp. 10–15.

cups of precious metals which fifteenth-century painters and sculptors depicted in scenes of the Adoration of the Magi. While many glasses of similar shape came from the Venetian workshops, this blue goblet does not follow exactly their model. The differences are minute but clearly discernible: a greater flare to the rim; a threaded, not a serrated, flange around the base of the bowl; a shorter stem; a conical foot that is smooth, not ribbed. The floral and flame patterns, painted to leave a broad area of the bowl unadorned, are vastly unlike the scenic representations depicted on Venetian goblets of the same period.

# 2

## CATALUÑA AND NEIGHBOURING REGIONS

As the sixteenth century began, the glass-blowers of Cataluña were about to enter an era of great splendour. For the next one hundred and fifty years, the products of their blowpipes were true works of art, never again in the history of Spanish glassmaking to be surpassed in beauty and variety. These craftsmen were not to any extent innovators, for, as practical men, they learned to supply their customers with the most popular glassware of its day, that done in Venetian style. Nevertheless, the Catalan glasses 'à la façon de Venise' show individuality in colouring and in shapes which are truly Spanish, revealing in their clean, firm lines an aversion to daintiness and cluttered detail, and reminding us always of the skilled workmanship necessary for their creation.

Contemporary historians, geographers and travellers recognized the beauty of this glass and its similarity to the Venetian, some of them going so far as to assert that it surpassed the Venetian. 'The glass that today is made in Venice is considered excellent', wrote Pere Gil, 'but . . . in many ways, that made in Barcelona and other parts of Cataluña is better . . . and so Cataluña is praised and esteemed for its glass, and boxes [of it] are shipped to Castilla, the West Indies, France, Italy and elsewhere.'[1] Contemporary authors even claimed that it went to Venice, but this statement may have been no more than a patriotic boast.[2]

Recognition of Catalan glass came from Ferdinand the Catholic in 1503 when he sent one hundred and forty-eight glasses from Barcelona to Queen Isabel, who was then residing at Alcalá de Henares. They were additions

---

[1] Gudiol Ricart, *op. cit.*, pp. 155, 157, *tr.*
[2] 'Our glass has been carried as far as Venice . . .' (in F. Santos, *La verdad en el potro, y el Cid resucitado*, Madrid, 1686, p. 36, *tr.*)

to a collection of more than two hundred and sixty pieces already housed in the palace, all of which she later willed to Granada Cathedral for the Royal Chapel. In 1526, Andrea Navagero, gentleman of Murano and Venetian ambassador to Charles V, mentioned having seen these glasses in the cathedral sacristy, together with Isabel's books, medals, and tapestries.[1] All the glasses and most of the other gifts have since disappeared, probably sold by order of Charles V, as were the Queen's jewels.

To the lady-in-waiting, Violante de Albión, we are indebted for her vivid descriptions of these glasses, written during May of the year 1503 with such telling detail that each piece is brilliantly pictured.[2] Many glasses were blue or purple, although green appeared occasionally; certain examples were blown in 'enamels' of white, golden-brown, purple or blue, indicating milk glass and other opaque colours. Not infrequently, glasses of two colours would be combined in the same piece: clear uncoloured glasses might have covers, handles and feet that were of blue, purple or green, or their rims might be encircled with threading of blue or opaque white. Mottled glass was described as 'enamelled to resemble chalcedony'. This imitation of semi-precious stones — onyx, agate and chalcedony — was in a tradition traceable to Roman glass manufacture, a technique revived by the Venetians during the late-fifteenth century.

Lady Violante attempted to differentiate between two types of gilding, the kind called 'dorado', which seems to mean solid areas of gold, and 'dorado de oro molido'. By the latter phrase, she probably referred to the technique in which flecks of gilt were spattered on the surface of the glass. Gold-flecked glass used ornamentally for prunts and trailed decoration may be seen still on Catalan glasses (Plates 12, 16).

Painted designs embellished these glasses from Barcelona, and the motifs described were those of the 'estilo Isabel', a combination of late Gothic, Mudejar and early Renaissance styles which flourished in Spain toward the end of her reign. Coats of arms and devices adorned several glasses: a purple plate displayed the royal arms in gilt encircled by foliage; the armorial bearing of a castle, for Castilla, was repeated around a blue box, appearing also on a tall vase of purple glass with gold-flecked handles. Angels and human beings, animals and birds occurred frequently, painted in white and coloured enamels. Sometimes the figures were framed by gilt medallions, or they stood against a foliage background, as for example, boys and birds among the green branches that spread over a purple and

---

[1] A. Navagero, *Viaje a España del magnífico señor Andres Navagero (1524–1526)* ... tr ... de José María Alonso Gamo, Valencia, 1951, p. 71.

[2] Gudiol Ricart, *op. cit.* pp. 142–54, note 72; the entire inventory of glasses is given in this reference.

gold goblet. A grotesque creature decorating a blue basin was described as a bird with the face of a man.

Inscriptions having been a favourite decoration during the Middle Ages, it is not surprising to find them on glasses listed in the Queen's inventory. Mostly they were of a religious nature, written in gothic letters. The 'Ave Maria' occurs several times, and a purple vase decorated with a hunting scene bore the words, 'Anima mea', on the collar. A blue goblet, partly gilt and beaded with coloured dots, displayed beneath its rim the words, 'Domine en manus tuas encomendo espiritu meo'. Pieces ornamented with 'Moorish' letters suggest Mudejar influence, the work of Muslims living within Christian territory. A box combined these characters with gilt rings and enamelled pearling, and a covered jar had 'round the collar Moorish letters in white enamel'. Three more glasses of blue or purple displayed white 'Moorish' lettering, the calligraphy painted above diaper patterns of stars, flowerlets or little pearls in white and gold.

The secondary motifs and all-over ground patterns of Queen Isabel's glasses are important enough to mention, because their very names point them out as typical of Gothic decoration. Most frequently noted are backgrounds sprinkled with 'little buttons', 'dots', or 'seeds that resemble pearls', 'drops of enamel like tears' and 'small enamel stones like turquoises'. Combined with these imitation gem stones are white stars, flames, golden roses and flowerlets. The 'arches gilt to look like fish scales', as described by Lady Violante, may have been the scale pattern which is seen on so many Venetian glasses dating from the same period. The woven patterns of gold brocades and a motif of peacock feathers decorated others of Queen Isabel's treasures.

A great variety of shapes is indicated in the inventory: plates, bowls and trays; jugs for water and wine; covered goblets and wineglasses; hand basins and ewers; flower vases and covered jars for sweets; wine flasks, some of them gourd-shaped, salt dishes and cruets. There were candlesticks, one of gold-flecked purple glass for the altar, and a green jar with a twisted collar and four spouts, undoubtedly the Catalan 'almorratxa' or rose-water sprinkler. If fashioned in a curious manner, a pedestal or a handle was noted as shaped like a serpent's head, a human hand or a bird.

Isabel's daughter Juana accumulated during her lifetime many glasses of artistic merit, some enamelled and gilt or fashioned to imitate jasper, chalcedony and other semi-precious stones. Detailed descriptions of them appear in an inventory of her possessions drawn up at the time of her death. Among the lot may have been glasses purchased in 1503 by her husband Philip the Handsome, duke of Burgundy, when he visited a glass furnace in the suburbs of Barcelona. There he watched the blowing of fine 'crystal' glasses and thought them very beautiful.[1]

During the reign of the Emperor Charles (1516–56), the glass industry of Barcelona stood up against strong competition from the glasses of Murano and the Venetian-type 'crystals' of other countries. Outside Cataluña, Spain provided an active market, continuing well into the seventeenth century, for the exportation of these objects. Purchased for the households of noble families, Venetian glasses penetrated to regions as remote from their source as Extremadura and Galicia. In 1528, the death of the Marquis of Priego and Count of Feria occasioned the recording of his possessions at Zafra, when it became known that his glass tableware from Venice included wineglasses with gilt handles, fruit dishes of blue, gilt or frosted glass and goblets decorated with the arms of Portugal.[2] At Santiago de Compostela in 1549, the Countess of Altamira owned more than one hundred and twenty-four pieces of Venetian glass — goblets, jugs, decanters and wine kegs — and eleven rosaries with Venetian glass beads.[3]

The third duke of Alburquerque collected in his castle at Cuéllar a rare treasure of glass, much of it from Venice, although some came from Barcelona and Cadalso. The richest of these objects listed in 1560 had engraved, enamelled and gilt decorations.[4] Other sixteenth-century collections of glass were equally cosmopolitan. Francisca Ruiz de Castejón in 1586 owned pieces imported from Venice and Florence, where Venetian-style glass was being made, as well as products from the Spanish glass furnaces at Barcelona, Figueras, Valencia and Cadalso. Various types of workmanship characterized the forty-four pieces of Venetian glass that belonged in 1599 to Diego Fernández de Córdoba. This Knight-Commander of Calatrava and Equerry to the King also counted among his household goods many Castillian glasses and over two hundred from Barcelona.[5]

Aware of how highly their products were esteemed throughout Europe,

[1] J. Ferrandis Torres, *Datos documentales para la historia del arte español*, Madrid, 1943, vol. 3, p. [171]–375; A. de Lalaing, lord of Montigny, *Voyage de Philippe le Beau en Espagne* (in *Collection des voyages des souverains des Pays-Bas*, pub. par M. Gachard, Brussels, 1876, vol. 1, p. 257).

[2] *Series de los mas importantes documentos del archivo y biblioteca del Exmo. señor duque de Medinaceli* [Madrid, 1915] vol. 1, p. 159.

[3] *Testamento e inventario de D.ª Ana de Toledo, condesa de Altamira.—año 1546* (in Academia Gallega, Coruña, *Colección de documentos historicos*, 1931, vol. 2, pp. 14, 16).

[4] *Inventario del moviliario . . . del Excmo. señor D. Beltrán de la Cueva, tercer duque de Alburquerque, A.º 1560* (in *Revista de archivos, bibliotecas y museos*, Madrid, 31 March, 1883, año 9, pp. 101–2).

[5] C. Pérez Pastor, *Noticias y documentos relativos a la historia y literatura españolas*, Madrid, 1914, vol. 2, pp. 224–5; 1910, vol. 1, pp. 311, 314 (R. Academia Española, Madrid, *Memorias*, vols. 11, 10).

Italian glassmen accepted tempting offers to blow Venetian-style glass in countries far from home. Workers from Venice, Altare and Brescia crossed the Alps to set up furnaces in France and the Netherlands. By the middle of the sixteenth century, as the archives and registers of their native cities prove, they had established themselves in the Iberian peninsula.[1] The government of Venice enacted statutes in 1549 to penalize those who refused to return home from foreign countries and gave orders for the improvement of wages and labour conditions on Murano island. Some of the wandering artisans came back, but numbers of them ignored the edicts and others, later on, defied banishment and the galleys to venture forth on a similar quest.

Of the Italian glass-blowers for whom Spain was the goal, the names of several have been recorded, not always with reference to the locale in which they settled. The wanderers seem to have preferred glass centres in Castilla, yet several of these foreigners settled within the Catalan domain. Among them was a member of the renowned Barovier family of Murano. This Domingo Barovier established himself at Palma de Mallorca in 1600 and five years later claimed to have brought the art of making Venetian-style 'crystals' to the island. Pleading extreme poverty, he requested the Mallorcan council to authorize him a sum of money as recompense for his services in teaching native glass-blowers. So useful had his instructions proved, said he, that it was no longer necessary to import glass from Venice or elsewhere. The plea that he had risked exile, death or slavery for his sojourn in Mallorca left the councillors unmoved, for they failed to grant his petition. Disappointed, he left the island and in 1608, set up a glass furnace at El Escorial in the Castillian province of Madrid.[2]

Wanderers previous to Domingo Barovier were probably responsible for teaching Catalan glass-blowers their carefully guarded methods of working in the Venetian manner. The master craftsmen of Barcelona must have seen and copied Venetian importations which arrived abundantly at their port-city. By the time Philip II came to the throne of Spain, Barcelona glass blown and decorated in Venetian style had increased enormously in popularity. Important collections like that of the King included about as many Barcelona glasses as importations. Listed among his household possessions at El Pardo Palace in 1564 were three hundred and twenty

[1] H. Schuermans, *Verres 'façon de Venise' fabriqués aux Pays-Bas* (in Belgium, Commissions Royales d'Art et d'Archéologie, *Bulletin*, 1890, 29ᵉ année, p. 140).

[2] E. Fajarnés y Tur, *Sobre invenciones industriales antiguas en Mallorca. XIV.–Fabricació de cristall de Venetia per Domingo Barrouier (1605)* (in Sociedad Arqueológica Luliana, Palma, *Boletín*, 1895, vol. 6, p. 191); Pérez Pastor, *op. cit.*, vol. 2, p. 244.

B. *Flask, with trailed threading and chain pattern.*
*Probably María (Almería), late sixteenth century. Ht.* $6\frac{9}{16}$ *in.* (16.7 *cm.*)
*The Hispanic Society of America, New York*
(*See page* 55)

Venetian glasses and two hundred and sixty-three glasses of Barcelona. His fourth queen, Anne of Austria, acquired during her lifetime three hundred additional glasses from Barcelona.[1]

When Philip visited the city in 1585, the historian of the royal journey, a Netherlander named Henry Cock, commented that glassmaking was a principal occupation among the people.[2] The guild of glass-blowers still played a prominent part in public life and supplied two members to the council. In 1594, they broke away from their former companions, the esparto-weavers, and formed a separate brotherhood under the protection of Saint Michael. New regulations drawn up at this time specifically set the term of apprenticeship for a glass-blower to four years and prohibited an unlicensed person from making glass. Street vendors henceforward would have to pay the guild for licences to sell glass, and individuals wishing to open up shops had to obtain permission from the guild. Soon the guild officers began to realize their power as an increasingly influential body, and on occasion they did not hesitate to defy the Barcelona council.[3]

The annual glass fairs continued throughout the sixteenth century, although by 1564 the glassmen rebelled and begged the city magistrates to omit the traditional display. As the reason for their request, they claimed a loss of profit due to the excessive breakage of their wares. Evidently the glass fairs brought so much prestige to the city that the magistrates would not dispense with the festivities. Indeed, they issued a writ against the glass-blowers and required them to hold the customary fair on the next New Year's Day. The only cause considered sufficiently important to cancel the fair was the period of national mourning in 1599 for the death of Philip II. Celebrations could be an excuse to repeat the fair, as when the Duke and Duchess of Osuna, returning from Naples on the fifth of January 1585, disembarked at Barcelona.[4]

Contemporary opinions of Barcelona glass suggest that the favourite variety from the sixteenth century onwards was crystal. The Flemish chronicler of Philip the Handsome's journey through Spain in 1503 referred to the glasses of Barcelona as 'voires de cristallin très beaus'.[5] Another early instance of the word 'crystal', as applied to Catalan glass,

---

[1] F. J. Sánchez Cantón, *El primer inventario del palacio de El Pardo (1564)* (in *Archivo español de arte y arqueología*, Madrid, 1934, vol. 10, pp. 73–5); B. Bassegoda y Amigó, *Santa María de la Mar*, Barcelona, 1925, vol. 1, p. 381.

[2] E. Cock, *Relación del viaje hecho por Felipe II, en 1585 . . . pub . . . por Alfredo Morel-Fatio y Antonio Rodríguez Villa*, Madrid, 1876, pp. 127–8.

[3] Gudiol Ricart, *op. cit.*, pp. 46–7.

[4] Gudiol Ricart, *op. cit.*, pp. 47–8.

[5] Lalaing, *op. cit.*, p. 257.

appears in the inventory of a nobleman of Barcelona who in 1510 owned a cruet of 'crystal or crystalline glass'. Later in the century, Pere Gil described the finest grade of Catalan glass as 'vidre cristalli'. One historian in the early seventeenth century wrote that the glass of Barcelona was as fine and transparent as the glass of Venice, exceeding it in delicacy of designs.[1]

Barcelona holds an even better claim than Murano to the distinction of having been the first glass centre to make crystal. Catalan inventories dating back at least to 1389 used the term 'blanco' to describe glasses blown obviously of a transparent and nearly colourless metal. By the mid-fifteenth century the crystal-clear glasses of Barcelona were considered more valuable than other varieties.[2] To produce this crystal the Catalans undoubtedly used the famous barilla of Alicante, a substance known to them long before foreigners had become acquainted with its desirable qualities.

After the middle years of the sixteenth century, Spanish patrons ordered little else than crystal from glassworkers of the Barcelona region. Venetian-type crystals being all the rage, Catalan glass-blowers became ever more skilful in their imitations, although they maintained certain techniques of decoration traditional to their own work. First among their forms of ornament was enamel-painting, which the Venetians had relinquished gradually. The Spaniards, slow to give up customs satisfactory in the past, kept alive the demand for enamelled glass until the mid-seventeenth century. References in inventories to 'painted glass' or to 'glass painted in divers colours' are frequent, while occasionally one sees listed a glass described in more detail, like the covered drinking vessel 'painted in green, gold, and white' that belonged in 1581 to a lady of Vich. Of the many glass lamps at El Pardo Palace in 1564, thirty-four were said to have been 'splashed with white enamel'.[3]

What these enamelled glasses were and how they looked is known from surviving examples. Most of this comparatively small group belong to the Museos de Arte of Barcelona. Several private collections in Cataluña still retain an individual object or two, and museums elsewhere are fortunate if they have a single example. So rare are they that not one of these glasses has appeared on the art market for years. Those in the Victoria and Albert

---

[1] J. M. Roca, *Inventaris* (in R. Academia de Buenas Letras, Barcelona, *Boletín*, 1930, vol. 14, p. 293); Gudiol Ricart, *op. cit.*, pp. 155, 51–2; L. Sánchez Costa, *La península á principios del siglo XVII* (in *Revue hispanique*, Paris, 1915, vol. 34, p. 477).

[2] *Tarifa impuesta* . . . [*1453*] *op. cit.*, pp. 141–2.

[3] Gudiol Ricart, *op. cit.*, p. 51; Sánchez Cantón, *op. cit.*, p. 75. The white enamel splashes on these glass lamps may have been marvered into the surface to give it the mottled appearance of marble or another stone.

and the British Museums were acquired between 1869 and 1914; and the three belonging to The Hispanic Society of America were purchased in 1911 and 1912, a vase (Colour plate A) and a goblet bowl having come from the sale of the famous collection of Adalbert von Lanna at Prague. The entire group of these enamelled glasses can be dated within a period from the mid-sixteenth century to the year 1638.

The glasses, although obviously intended to be crystal clear, have a faint grey or yellow tinge. They are rather thick-walled, blown thus for strength, since they later required annealing to fuse the enamels. This process has been explained by a sixteenth-century historian, who wrote, 'Crystal glasses, when completely finished, are painted with green, gold, and other colours and returned to the furnace . . . for annealing; and that colouring remains fixed so fast that it can rarely, if ever, be separated.'[1] The gilt was unfired, produced by painting an oil or a varnish mixed with a drying agent on the glass, then pressing gold leaf against the sticky substance. The gilt was dried with artificial heat, but not fired, and burnished to give it brilliance.

The contemporary references to green and white enamels imply that they were the dominant colours, a characteristic true of existing glasses of this kind. The gold that originally shone so brilliantly has worn away and dimmed with the centuries, but the greens and yellows remain bright. Less frequently there occur blue, violet, grey, terracotta red and sepia. The enamels were applied freehand with a full brush to the exterior of the glass, so that the designs cover almost the entire surface. This technique, comparable with the Syrian, caused the opaque enamels to stand out in relief and so reflect light with a sparkling radiance.

Enamelling on these Catalan glasses, applied in the Islamic manner, fills every available space so that little of the glass itself is visible. Green trees and plants cover the surfaces – leaves on spiralled stems or upright stalks, cypress and orange trees, thistle plants or fern fronds, bluebells and lilies-of-the-valley. An ovate leaf and a circular blossom with furred edges are two motifs commonly seen on these glasses. Perched on the greenery are white birds, their wings half-extended as though arrested momentarily in flight. Decorated with typical background designs are a dish that has flamelike rays around the brim (Plate 9B) and a vase (Plate 4) that displays a cross potent and fringed dots encircled by lacy scallops in green and yellow. The heraldic motif was probably intended for the arms of the military Order of the Holy Sepulchre. This vase and one in New York (Colour plate A) belong to a small number having a shape that is basically

---

[1] Gil, as quoted in Gudiol Ricart, *op. cit.*, p. 156, *tr.*

Syrian. All have flattened bodies like pilgrim flasks, and the collars either swell in a bulbous form or flare to the shape of an inverted cone.

Renaissance motifs were sparingly included in the repertory of the Catalan glass-enameller, although he was working at a time when patterns of trophies, urns, masks and cupids were greatly favoured. No such fantasies came from his brush, for he painted flowers, shrubs, beasts and humans as things that he actually saw. The hunt theme depicting lean hounds that race after a stag persisted long in glass decoration. During the last quarter of the sixteenth century these animals, taken from their accustomed forest setting, were combined with the only perceptibly Renaissance design that one can find. A footed dish (Plate 5A–B) shows the animals above a swag enamelled in yellow and green to represent fruit and leaves tied into long festoons. The painting is done without perspective, so that the figures are flat with no modelling in light and shadow and with incised lines to suggest the animals' contours. In painting the Hispanic Society's vase the same two-dimensional style was used. Twice repeated on the smoky yellow glass are the figures of a lady and a gentleman dressed in the Court attire fashionable about 1580.

A characteristic shape among glasses of the Barcelona region is the covered jar with walls either cylindrical or curved like an inverted bell and raised on a conical foot (Plate 17). Around an enamelled jar of this kind (Plate 8) are painted bands of bluebells, which border a panel enclosing white birds perched on stalks of apple-green foliage. Domed lids with knob handles originally covered all such vessels, which were probably the sweetmeat jars listed in inventories as holding conserves and fragrant liquids. In 1594, a Mallorcan lady had several containing lemon preserve, rose sugar and other sweets.

Vessels for pouring wine, water and oil were common in sixteenth-century households, recorded by the names of 'gerro', 'aiguamanil' and 'setrill'. Some idea of these forms is gained from a glass that has the classic lines of an Italian Renaissance ewer wrought in silver or gold (Plate 6). The enamelled decoration adds to its Italianate look, since the broad bands of green foliage on a powdering of yellow dots are based on a Venetian pattern. This piece has a rich and brilliant appearance, achieved by the gilt handle and the gold, yellow and blue stripes between the leaf scrolls.

Unique among the enamelled glasses is a vessel shaped like an aspersory, or holy-water bucket with a bail handle (Plate 7B). The base and sides are painted with a hunting scene of white hounds running beneath trees where birds perch high in the branches. Similar ecclesiastical vessels were no novelty to the Venetians; quantities of them have survived to the present day, many in the Museo Vetrario at Murano. In Cataluña, also, this form was decidedly popular, listed in inventories under the name of 'caldereta'. Queen Isabel had at least half-a-dozen, one described as resembling a bucket, of clear glass with a twisted blue handle. Twenty-one Venetian glasses of this shape belonged to Philip II, and a dozen of them, some with gilt handles, came to him from the workshops of Barcelona.[1]

Religious communities directed the glassworkers to mark enamelled glasses with the insignia of their orders. On several objects still existing there is painted, usually in white, the monogram 'I H S' with a cross rising above the 'H' and a triad of nails below. In this manner it is represented on a fruit dish, surrounded by sprays of light green foliage (Plate 7A). A sanctuary lamp (Plate 9A) has the same monogram, the symbol adopted by the Society of Jesus after its foundation in 1534 by Ignatius Loyola. The Maltese cross, sign of the Knights of Malta, marks one serving dish, formerly in the Juan Prats collection, now in the Instituto Amatller, Barcelona. These military monks known also as the Knights of Saint John of Jerusalem were liberal clients of the Barcelona glass-blowers. A vase displaying the cross of the Order of the Holy Sepulchre (Plate 4) has already been described, and in addition there should be mentioned a covered ewer, now in the Macaya collection, Barcelona, that was found in the Convent of Santa Clara at Palma de Mallorca. The escutcheon of the Monastery of Montserrat, a carpenter's saw cutting through mountain peaks, identifies a sanctuary lamp in the Instituto Amatller with that religious house. A lamp belonging to the Museos de Arte at Barcelona reveals even more of its history through the enamelled decoration: on it appear the date 1638, the Franciscan symbol – the Cross rising above clouds and the arm of Christ crucified crossed over the arm of Saint Francis of the Stigmata – as well as the name of the Abbot Bartomeu Amat. Still another lamp in the same collection bears a heart pierced by arrows and inscribed 'A I', and on the opposite side, the escutcheon and name of the prelate F. Marimón, probably Felipe Marimón of Mallorca, who became bishop of Ampurias and lived until 1613.

Like the Venetians, the glass-blowers of Barcelona were experts during the sixteenth century in producing frosted or ice-glass. The methods used to obtain a fissured surface were probably two: either the 'gather' was plunged into water directly after a preliminary blowing and smoothed by further heating and blowing, or it was rolled over glass splinters, then fused and smoothed by reheating. Known in Castilla as 'vidrio helado' and in Cataluña as 'vidre gelat', this frosted glass sparkles like crushed ice. Philip

[1] Sánchez Cantón, *op. cit.*, p. 74.

II liked it so well that his palace of El Pardo alone contained sixty-five pieces from Venice, among them covered goblets and flutes, aspersories and a decanter; there was also an indeterminate number of frosted glasses from Barcelona.[1] To a Catalan workshop may be attributed a Renaissance jug (Plate 10) of pale straw-coloured glass in helmet shape, its crested handle pincered and bent into reverse curves. Other examples of ice-glass are fruit bowls and delicate wine glasses raised on baluster stems. Occasionally one finds a dish that combines a frosted surface in the centre with diamond-point engraving round the brim.

Spaniards began importing engraved glasses from Venice during the second half of the sixteenth century. From Murano the art of the diamond-point spread to Flanders, Spain and England, where artists learned how to scratch lightly into the fragile, Venetian-type crystal, producing Renaissance designs in fine, shallow lines. To the craftsmen of Barcelona have been accredited several glasses ornamented with flowers, birds and acanthus foliage drawn in outline and filled in with faint hatchings. A design of this kind encircles the brim of a serving dish (Plate 11A–B) that has the additional ornamentation of a trailed chain and milled bands.

A variety of glassware that greatly interested the Spaniards was crystal striped in opaque white, which is now called *latticinio*. In sixteenth-century Spain it was referred to as 'lo rayado a la manera de Venecia' (that striped in the manner of Venice). A drinking glass in 1581 was described as having white lines, 'bavedora de vidre ab ses vies blancas' (a drinking glass with its white lines) and another glass, which belonged to a Mallorcan doctor in 1616, had white stripes, 'bauedora ab rretxas blancas' (a drinking glass with white stripes).[2] The Venetian method of obtaining this effect was to stand canes of opaque white glass upright in a cylindrical mould and to blow a 'gather' of crystal between them. The mass was marvered to embed the white canes further and then was blown to the desired shape, the white appearing as flat stripes through the crystal.

The glass-blowers in Spain, particularly in Cataluña, quite successfully imitated *latticinio* and, using much the same method, produced also a kind of glass in which the white canes stood out in relief from the crystal. This type of striping extends up the bowls of wineglasses (Plates 12, 13) and round the knops of stemmed glasses (Plates 16, 24) and ornaments the cover and bowl of a sweetmeat jar (Plate 17) in the Instituto Amatller. On certain shapes, opaque white stripes were combined with bosses or prunts

---

[1] Sánchez Cantón, *op. cit.*, pp. 73–4.
[2] Gudiol Ricart, *op. cit.*, p. 50; G. Llabrés, *Testament del doctor en medicina, Joan Binimelis, prevera* (in Societat Arqueológica Luliana, Palma, *Bolletí*, 1916, vol. 16, p. 189).

with moulded designs, usually of clear blue or gold-flecked glass (Plates 12, 14A–B, 15A, 16). An 'almorratxa', a characteristic shape of Cataluña (Plate 16), illustrates several kinds of glass decoration: vertical ribs of milk-glass, white threading to link the four spouts, a reticulated edging of pincered glass around the brim and prunts of gold-flecked glass below the curved spouts. Catalan references to 'almorratxas' date back at least to the fourteenth century, when vessels of this shape decorated with enamel-painting were imported from Damascus. During the sixteenth century the glass-blowers of Barcelona regularly made 'almorratxas', and vendors sold them all over the region. Many were ordered from Venice as well. Listed among the Venetian glasses belonging to Philip II in 1564 were 'four flasks of almorratxa shape', and the Duke of Alburquerque had a 'Venetian glass almorratxa of small size'.[1]

Diagonal stripes of *latticinio* were obtained by giving a twist to the bulb of glass while it hung pliable on the blow-pipe. This process was used for a wineglass (Plate 20) of flamboyant shape, with a constricted bowl and tooled handles. Twisted stripes also run through a wineglass of a less complicated form (Plate 21) that stands on a high baluster stem. Bands of opaque white trailed horizontally around a gather of glass, followed by blowing and 'combing', produced the scalloped pattern seen on a cruet (Plate 23A) of Venetian style. Similar cruets, which may have served as Eucharistic vessels, are in the collections of several museums, among them the Victoria and Albert and the Hermitage at Leningrad. Combed *latticinio* did well for representing the wooden staves of a wine barrel on small glass containers that Catalans called 'barralets' (Plate 23B). These kegs were filled usually with choice brandies. Glass striped or scalloped in *latticinio* remained in high favour until the end of the eighteenth century.

Venetians developed even greater skill in the manufacture of this kind of glass by using canes that had been previously prepared from a combination of opaque and transparent glasses drawn out and then twisted. These canes of twisted threads produced vertical lacy patterns when embodied in a gather of transparent glass. Catalan glass-blowers, less skilful in making threaded canes, at first limited their work to solid white stripes, not undertaking the more difficult lacy design until the eighteenth century. Even then, the canes were in fairly simple patterns resembling twisted braids (Plates 33A, 34).

Another form of decoration, although it affects the surface, is allied closely to the form itself namely, bas-relief patterns obtained by moulds.

---

[1] Sánchez Cantón, *op. cit.*, p. 74; *Inventario . . . del . . . tercer duque de Alburquerque*, p. 102.

While not commonly used to shape entire vessels, the two-part metal mould occasionally served the glass-blowers of sixteenth-century Cataluña in this way. A gather was blown thinly into a mould of this kind, which could then be opened to remove the glass. Moulds enabled the glassmaker to turn out decanters decorated with a frieze of dancers (Plate 24) and other bottles formed like pine-cones or bunches of grapes. After the mould-blown paraison was removed from the mould, but still attached to the blow-pipe, a hollow knop and a conical foot were fixed to its base. A pontil was next attached to the underside of the foot to hold the glass so that a long neck might be drawn out and the decanter finally detached from the blow-pipe. Written records of the period mention pine-cones, calabashes and chestnuts as shapes for these decanters, which contained wine, brandy, rose-water and other liquids. Another aid to the workman was the pattern-mould into which glass was blown, then removed and expanded by further blowing. A bowl and a spouted vessel with fluted bases and free-blown walls (Plates 25A, 26) demonstrate the results of this technique, one that became ever more common as the seventeenth century advanced. The diamond-shaped projections arranged in diaper over the outer surface of a cylindrical glass (Plate 25B) were probably achieved by blowing the glass into an indented mould. Apparently free-blown, a bucket-shaped bowl (Plate 27A) must have been indented by a tool to give it a dimpled surface. A bucket with a twisted bail-handle (Plate 30) was blown in a ribbed mould.

Of all the Venetian-style glasses made by the Barcelonese, the wineglass best shows their versatility. During the sixteenth century and through the early years of the seventeenth, the shapes of these objects had a diversity of outline and an elegance of proportion that delight the eye. The bowls, flowing in graceful curves, take on the forms of trumpet, thistle, cone or bell. Some wineglasses have small round bowls that flare out to wide brims (Plates 12, 13, 28, 29); some are blown from plain crystal (Plates 28b, 29a); others are *latticinio*-striped, or engraved with the diamond-point or frosted; some show the rippled surfaces obtained by tooling, twisting and by using a pattern-mould (Plate 28a); others depend for their beauty on melting curves of great simplicity (Plate 28b). Handles, pincered flat and rippling like ribbons, ornament many sixteenth-century wineglasses (Plates 18–20), yet the glass-blowers of the Barcelona region show less exuberance in this decorative work than did the imitators of Venice in Flanders, Germany and the Netherlands. Among Catalan glasses, the fantastic Venetian-type stems designed as writhing dragons or serpents and as intricate wings of trailed and pinched glass are totally lacking. The hollow knops used in the stems of Catalan wineglasses often take the form of lion's-head masks, produced by blowing the gather into two-part moulds (Plates 13, 28b). Perhaps the earliest form of stem was a hollow cone blown from a separate gather and attached to the bowl (Plates 3, 12). The more usual stems were the hollow tube and the solid rod (Plates 18, 29); plain, inverted balusters of varying proportions (Plates 21, 28a) were common also. Fanciful stems were composed of clustered glass rods, some angularly bent with little discs attached to each crook. These prunts, stamped with lion's-head masks, raspberries and flowers were ornamental appendages well liked during the sixteenth century.

Aside from the shapes already considered and the glasses associated usually with table settings, such as footed dishes or comports, plates, bowls and drinking glasses, a few strange objects came from the blowpipes of the Catalan workers. In studying them, the observer is led to believe that the glassmaker amused himself in his off time or that he hoped to ensnare a buyer with his whimsy. A 'Spanish toque' (Plate 14A) may be dated from its style as having been made between the years 1585 and 1595. The crown is marked with opaque white stripes in relief to represent pleats, and the broad brim is turned back and held in place with a blue glass button. Possibly the maker intended that the hat be inverted and used as a small vase. An ornamental cock (Plate 22) is among the best of the animal pieces that remain to us. The entire body of the bird and its tail feathers are formed from a single gather of *latticinio* glass blown, twisted and tooled into shape. Its eyes, beak and comb and the serrated edges of its wings and tail feathers are done in cobalt-blue glass. Another invention is a sabot of *latticinio*-striped glass (Plate 15B), supposedly a jewel box. These amusing objects were undoubtedly the sort of thing that a seventeenth-century gentleman of Piedmont meant when he wrote, 'In this city of Barcelona the glass trinkets are most admirable.'[1] On the Calle de la Vidriería, the Street of the Glass Shops, all sorts of curiosities could be bought, not only drinking vessels of enamelled, gilt and coloured glasses but also glass jewels and ornaments, chains, buttons and rings. In 1603 this prodigal display astonished a French visitor, familiar as he was with the fashionable offerings of the Paris shops.[2]

Some attention should be given to the general workmanship shown in Catalan glasses of this period. All of them exemplify superior qualities in colour, stability of metal, variety of shape and multiplicity of techniques.

[1] D. del Final, *Viage de la famosa villa de Madrid . . . a la ciudad de Roma*, Madrid [1664?] *f* 3, *tr.*

[2] B. Joly, *Voyage . . . en Espagne (1603–1604)* (in *Revue hispanique*. Paris, 1909, vol. 20, p. 476).

They lack the diaphanous texture of the Murano glasses, nicety of line and decoration, excessively refined shapes and minutely precise measurements. In place of these subtleties, the Catalan glasses offer straightforward traits that intensify their vigorous character – sturdiness based on somewhat thicker walls, strength gained by the absence of fussy details, a speedy flow of line, and minor irregularities of form. The finishing touches given to these glasses during the sixteenth and seventeenth centuries are worth noticing. The rims, and often the feet as well, were evened off with the shears and the sharp edges softened by reheating. Examples of folded edges to the feet are most usual, and covers with deep flanges, made to fit the openings securely, are the general rule.

★ ★ ★ ★ ★

Within the region of Cataluña, apart from Barcelona, were many towns, too numerous to mention individually, where the glass industry flourished. Most of these centres were situated in Barcelona province not far from the capital city. Others were scattered about in the provinces of Tarragona, Lérida, Gerona and the Roussillon.

The tradition of the Xatart family, renowned since the fourteenth century at Palau-del-Vidre (see pages 21, 24), was extended through 1538 by Joan Xatart, who had worked there since the year 1501 or longer. A glass-blower bearing the same family name worked at Prats de Molló during the early part of the century. Several glassmen from the Roussillon travelled southward to settle at Vich, as for example, Miquel Rossoli from the diocese of Narbonne, who married a girl of that town in 1528. Others from southern France are recorded as working at Vich throughout the sixteenth century.[1]

The history of glassmaking at Vallbona dates back to 1546, when Gabriel Badorc, a master of that town, agreed to teach a young Frenchman during the course of five years how to make glass according to the 'usage and custom of the said art in Barcelona'. During the seventeenth century a glass furnace was run by successive members of a family named Gralla. In 1673, a Pau Flor managed their factory. Until recent years a building called 'Can Flor', which may well have belonged to this glassworker, still existed. Quite evidently it had been a glass factory, because on its stone façade was carved a 'porró' or cruet and the date 1671. A glass acquired at the 'Can Flor' and now in the Museo Episcopal at Vich, is believed to have been made at the Flor furnace. This bottle, blown to a cylindrical shape typical of the early

---

[1] Gudiol Ricart, *op. cit.*, p. 48.

eighteenth century, is of clear, colourless glass decorated with *latticinio* stripes.[1]

A site known as 'Forn del Vidre' (Glass Furnace) once existed at Guardia de Montserrat where two master glassmen in 1606 agreed to instruct an apprentice for two years. Glass continued to be produced there until the latter part of the nineteenth century.[2] At Corbera de Llobregat, in front of the Romanesque church of Sant Pons, stood a large house traditionally named 'Forn del Vidre'. Legend locates a glass furnace at this site prior to the construction of the church. Excavations made there about thirty years ago by Gudiol and Macaya resulted in the discovery of a cullet heap containing a great quantity of fragments and vitrified material. Found also were the fragments of a crucible still containing the remains of fused glass metal. By piecing together the fragments of bottles, tumblers, plates and flasks, it was possible to identify glasses from the sixteenth to the eighteenth century, some moulded and others decorated with threads of *latticinio*. A dispute in 1610 between the Barcelona city council and the glass-blowers' guild confirms the presence of one or more factories at San Vicente dels Horts.[3]

By 1632, Mataró had become a more important glass centre than Barcelona proper and thus the Cardinal-Infante Fernando of Austria sailed four leagues from the Catalan capital to observe the glass-blowers of Mataró at work.[4] Even as late as 1678, when Spain was experiencing an industrial decline, an historian mentioned the glass of Barcelona province as being in great demand.[5] Seventeenth-century readers in the Dutch Netherlands learned from a German source, translated and printed in their own country, that Barcelona glasses were of exceptionally fine quality.[6]

★    ★    ★    ★    ★

The glassmakers' guild of Barcelona was very much in evidence during the seventeenth century. Powerful still, it had no fear of the city's governing body and refused in 1610 and again in 1627 to examine aspirants to the

---

[1] Gudiol Ricart, *op. cit.*, pp. 159–61.

[2] J. Mas, *Notes històriques del bisbat de Barcelona*, Barcelona, 1907, vol. 2, pp. 27–8.

[3] J. Gudiol Ricart and P. M. de Artíñano y Galdácano, *Vidrio: Resumen de la historia del vidrio; Catálogo de la colección Alfonso Macaya*, Barcelona, 1935, p. 65; Gudiol Ricart, *op. cit.*, pp. 52–3.

[4] D. de Aedo y Gallart, *El memorable y glorioso viaje del infante cardinal D. Fernando de Austria*, Amberes, 1635, pp. 8–9.

[5] E. Corbera, *Cataluña illustrada*, Naples, 1678, p. 67.

[6] J. de Laet, *Hispania, sive de regis hispaniae regnis et opibus commentarius*, Lugd: Batav; 1629, p. 16; idem, *Hispaniae et lusitaniae itinerarium*, Amstelodami, 1656, p. 302.

status of master. As punishment the council denied the guild its rightful privileges and ordered this decree to be cried through the streets to the sound of trumpets. The struggle in 1627 concerned the guildsmen's refusal to examine Felip Amiguet, who wished to build and operate a furnace at Barcelona. He sent his application to the guild, telling the glass-blowers that, although he was not a glassman himself, he wished his factory to produce all types of glass, both common and fine, the coloured varieties and Venetian-type crystals. These wares he intended to sell from a shop of his own. Amiguet claimed that his marriage to the daughter and heiress of a Barcelona glassmaker and his subsequent business associations enabled him to direct the master glassmen whom he planned to engage. He requested also that he might claim the title of master after he had operated his furnace and shop for four years. Months passed and the guild officials did not examine him. Tired of their defiance, the council itself granted Amiguet permission to choose the site for his furnace and make it ready for operation. He seized the opportunity and put all in readiness, only to have the guild fine him and warn him against opening his doors. The councillors admonished the glass-blowers that their action, if pursued, would cause the arrest of guild officials and all members. This threat failed to impress the glassworkers, and the bitter controversy ended in a two-years' suspension of the guild.[1]

★    ★    ★    ★    ★

Southwards in Valencia, a fair degree of activity enlivened the glass industry during the seventeenth century. Pere Boygues, master glassblower, sought permission in 1648 to construct a glass furnace in an impoverished area of the provincial capital. He claimed that his proposed furnace would stand far enough away from neighbouring houses for smoke and fire not to damage them. After inspecting the property, the city officials granted Boygues's request because more abundant quantities of glass were greatly needed. In 1689, a street in Valencia was called 'Forn del Vidre', as though a factory had long existed there. Until the end of the eighteenth century a glass furnace occupied a house that belonged to the Carroç family, and other establishments were operating within the city. Strangely enough, a glassworkers' guild seems not to have existed in Valencia. This lack, however, did not prevent them from taking part in celebrations like the tercentenary in 1755 of Saint Vincent Ferrer's canonization, when the glassmen contributed a processional float carrying a statue of the saint and a reproduction of a glass furnace. During the parade through the city,

[1] Gudiol Ricart, *op. cit.*, pp. 52–4.

glasses were blown and distributed to the spectators, although these souvenirs must have broken easily and soon, not having had proper annealing. A similar float was given by the glassmakers to honour the Virgin of los Desamparados.[1]

Evidently the glassware made at Valencia was rather ordinary and not in the Venetian manner, since a price list of merchandise of the early eighteenth century mentions among imports to the city 'glass from Venice, Barcelona or other foreign [centres], which is not made in the present Kingdom'.[2] Glassworkers tried to improve the quality of their wares toward the end of the century and to supply customers with crystals that would compare favourably with those from the royal factory of La Granja de San Ildefonso (see Chapter 5). In 1788, Pedro Fontvila, a Catalan, and Carlos Garcés became partner-owners of a factory at Valencia. After many experiments they succeeded in producing a clear, bright crystal of good quality from which to make chandeliers and blown vessels. They then petitioned for royal assistance that would enable them to produce window-panes, crystal, and other glasses of fine quality, both plain and decorated. King Charles III, knowing the scarcity of crystal-glass factories within the nation, consulted his council and the director of the Real Fábrica de Cristales. The decision was reached to permit Fontvila and Garcés and all other Spanish industrialists the privileges formerly reserved for the royal glass factory.[3] They could then buy raw materials untaxed at established low prices, ship their products free of export-duty to foreign countries and the dominions, and sell their glasses in every city of Spain.

Besides the provincial capital, several other Valencian towns produced glass during the eighteenth century. In 1791, there were six workshops in the Valencian region. Ollería was a principal centre, as was Salinas, where glassmaking had been a leading industry since the time of Muslim domination. Alcira, Busot and Alicante are all names to be associated with eighteenth-century glassmaking, especially Alicante for having continued to supply barilla to Spanish and foreign glass factories. Excavations made about 1892 brought to light glass fragments and cullet from several furnaces in Alicante. The products of these regional factories were window-panes, pharmacy bottles, lamps, bottles for holding wine, jugs and drinking vessels, blown or moulded in colourless or dark green glass.[4] Among the

---

[1] This Virgin, greatly revered, is the patroness of Valencia and protector of the needy, especially foundlings. (F. Almela y Vives, *La antigua industria del vidrio en Valencia*, Valencia, 1954, pp. 12–15).

[2] Almela y Vives, *op. cit.*, p. 5, *tr.*

[3] *Gazeta de Madrid*, 14 November, 1788, pp. 741–3.

[4] B. Espinalt y García, *Atlante español*, Madrid, 1784 vol. 8, pp. 321, 340; Almela y Vives, *op. cit.*, pp. 6, 18–20.

distinguishable shapes was the 'porró', like the footed example of transparent, colourless glass (Plate 33B), which has characteristics that suggest a Valencian source.

★　★　★　★　★

Aragón in the eighteenth century had its factories for common glass, although none of them could compete with Cataluña. At Peñalba and Jaulín, a dark glass was made, while at Utrillas and Vistabella the furnaces produced colourless glass of a low grade. Near the village of Crivillén furnaces operated to make crystal and coloured glasses, and Caspe also carried on its traditional industry of glassmaking. Early in the century an Aragonese glass-blower, Blas Rigal, travelled to Mallorca. While residing at Palma in 1719, he petitioned the city council for permission to build a furnace and workshop. These officials, after careful investigation of the chosen site, decided that Rigal's furnace, in addition to the number already in operation on the island, would better supply Mallorca's need for glasses. Along with the desired permit the glassmaker was issued a warning to construct a furnace with an underground chamber for the fuel so as to avoid the danger of fire.[1] In 1784, Aragonese workmen were encouraged to imitate the blown crystals made in the royal factory at San Ildefonso (see Chapter 5 ). Yearly prizes were offered by the Real Sociedad Aragonesa de Amigos del País for the three best groups of a dozen pieces, to be submitted by artisans from any factory in the region.[2]

★　★　★　★　★

The Catalan glass industry had begun to show a decline about 1650, and while slow in its spread, this decadence became all too noticeable in the next century. The delightful and luxurious glasses of the Renaissance were no longer created, although glasses in a debased Venetian style continued to be turned out at Barcelona. The blowers were content with producing objects of a popular and utilitarian nature and using their skill and energy to increase production rather than to improve quality and decorative style. Crystal glass took on an ashen-grey tonality. Blown shapes were reduced to a few popular objects used principally in taverns and kitchens, to commercial glasses found in pharmacies and chemists' shops, and to the toys, cheap jewellery and other trifles made from glass blown at the lamp.

Traditional Catalan shapes that came to the fore during the eighteenth

[1] Fajarnés, *Documents* (in Societat Arqueológica Luliana, Palma, *Bolletí*, September-October 1933, any 49, vol. 24, p. 418).
[2] *Gazeta de Madrid*, 13 February, 1784, p. 147.

century were the 'càntir', the 'porró', both of them drinking vessels for wine, and the 'almorratxa', or rose-water sprinkler. Decorated with *latticinio* and coloured threading, pincered cresting and other ornaments, the càntirs can be most fanciful, blown of uncoloured or *latticinio*-striped glass (Colour plate C, Plate 33A). They all have two spouts emerging from their spherical, ovoid or piriform bodies. Most of them are footed and topped by massive ring-handles bent from rods that are plain, grooved or threaded with coloured twists. Topping the handles are elaborate finials in the shapes of birds or flowers. Compared with the càntirs of Barcelona, those of southern France are plain and somewhat different in shape although they show characteristics of a style common to the region of Cataluña lying on both sides of the Pyrenees. The teapot-form with top opening and single curved spout (Plate 32A) is typical of these French-Catalan pieces; so is the constricted container (Plate 32B), the lower part of which is of a convenient size for grasping.

The almorratxa of the eighteenth century (Plate 31), not too different in shape from its predecessors (Plate 16) but with a narrow bottle-neck and shorter spouts, usually stands on a columnar stem and a circular foot. *Latticinio*-striped glass twisted to a helicoidal form is often used for the almorratxa, which always bristles with pincered crestings and drips with glass loops. The porró (Plates 34, 35) and the cruet, or 'setrill' as it is known in Cataluña, are much alike in shape, although their purposes are not the same. Probably derived from the medieval 'setrill' (Plate 1), the porró is a pear-shaped vessel, drawn to a bottla neck and finished with a flanged top. The glassworker pierced this single paraison in order to insert another, which he then drew out to an attenuated tube, forming a spout. To drink properly from the spout and not put it into the mouth, the countryman grasps the bottle around the neck and, holding it some distance away, pours the wine in an arc that will drain directly into the throat, a difficult performance for the uninitiated.

Drinking glasses of this period are so diverse in shape and style that they are not easily described. Some of them show that goblets and wineglasses of Venetian type must still have had their admirers. One of these glasses (Plate 27B) has an array of pincered discs emerging from the outer surfaces. More fashionable were the glasses in English style (Plate 39A–B). An uncoloured or crystal glass was chosen for the trumpet bowls, which were blown and set on hollow baluster stems, or for the bell-shaped bowls on solid, twisted columns. Mugs, used mostly in taverns for serving beer and cider (Plate 38A–B), closely resemble those made in other regions of Spain, especially in Andalucía.

Glass lamps for burning oil (Plates 36A–B, 37) were blown in many shapes, sometimes a circular tube that hung on the wall, or a standing cone with multiple spouts for the wicks, or a column with four spouts that could be carried about like a candlestick. Candlesticks to hold single candles were moulded in solid glass to resemble those wrought in silver or brass, and chandeliers were intricately constructed from numerous sections of pressed, free-blown or mould-blown glass.

Apart from table glass and lighting fixtures, the middle-class Catalan home might number among its furnishings many vases, trinkets and souvenirs. Vases having two decorative handles bristled with pincered cresting of uncoloured, blue or green glass (Plate 41). Fastened to the wall were holy-water stoups with *latticinio*-striped cups upheld by a network of glass cords (Plate 42); buckets and baskets (Plate 43) look ornamental but may have served as containers. The latter is a product of work at the lamp. Glass rods were heated until pliable, bent, and added tier on wavy tier to build up the desired structure. Over the top went a thick rod for a handle which was then ornately decorated with pincered cresting and a pert little bird.

Visitors to Catalan glass factories during the eighteenth century watched exhibitions of glass blowing and modelling performed for their especial benefit. The workmen followed wherever fancy led them and created gaudy càntirs, miniature animals, such as mice, birds and lizards (Plate 45A); and from glass rods came small hats and shoes, long-stemmed pipes (Plate 44) and knitting needles or spindles (Plate 45B) for the housewife. In enumerating the many glasses of this century, we should remember also those required by certain scientists and tradesmen. The glass-blowers of Cataluña supplied the chemist with retorts, stills and flasks; the apothecary needed glass bottles and albarellos for his shelves, and the perfumer stored liquid perfumes, potpourri and sachet powders in glass bottles.

Numerous centres within the region of Cataluña continued to prosper during the eighteenth century, despite the recession in the glass industry. Most prominent of those in the province of Barcelona, and thus nearest to the provincial capital, were Mataró, Villafranca del Panadés and Manresa. Mataró had two furnaces that upheld the old traditions in producing 'curious glasses' of fine quality and good workmanship, which were transported to other Spanish cities and shipped to foreign countries.[1] One of these factories continued to function until the mid-nineteenth century, its thirty workmen blowing goblets, bottles and flasks, moulding such objects as candlesticks (Plate 40), and making window-panes as well. It

[1] Espinalt, *op. cit.*, 1783, vol. 7, p. 86.

was from Mataró that Pedro Fontvila set out in 1788 to open a glass factory in Valencia. Other masters whose journeys led them from Cataluña, to the royal factory at San Ildefonso, were Ventura Sit (before 1728) and José Busquet (before 1780), but in what Catalan factory they were trained is not known.

The late years of the century were prosperous ones for the glass factory at Villafranca del Panadés, where the workers blew porrons, càntirs and holy-water stoups from crystal glass striped with *latticinio*.[1] By 1800 a factory at Manresa, directed by Jaime Ubach, was granted the privilege of placing the royal coat of arms over the entrance doors of the 'Fábrica de Vidrios Cristalinos de Bacarisas' and of selling crystal glasses, plate glass for coach windows and sheet glass in German-style at salesrooms in Madrid, Barcelona, Valencia and Zaragoza.[2]

In Gerona province, glass furnaces were active near Figueras and Cruilles and several were located in the massif called Las Gabarras. A farmhouse near La Junquera bears the name of 'Forn del Vidre', which seems to mean that it was in time past a glass factory. At La Bisbal, the glass drug jars, pharmacy bottles and phials of elongated cylindrical shapes that have been found in private homes indicate that they were products of a local glass factory. The city of Gerona, it is claimed, produced glass from the seventeenth to the late nineteenth century.[3] In the province of Lérida, about a league away from Almatret, stood a factory that once produced glass of superior quality. So many workers were employed there that the owners had to build a chapel on the premises in order that they might attend Mass on feast days.[4] The glassworkers of Cataluña kept their furnaces busy throughout the eighteenth century making the ordinary articles that local people needed for their homes and shops. Those more gifted craftsmen who sought to improve glass manufacture and its products found greater satisfaction by establishing themselves near Madrid, where their progressive efforts were sponsored by the King.

[1] F. Miquel y Badía, *Cerámica, joyas y armas*, Barcelona, 1882 [vol. 3] p. 129 (in his *La habitación*).
[2] *Gazeta de Madrid*, 28 February, 1800, p. 162.
[3] M. Oliva Prat, *Catálogo de los vidrios del Museo Arqueológico de Gerona* [Gerona] 1950, p. 15.
[4] Espinalt, *op. cit.*, 1783, vol. 6, pp. 63–4.

# 3

## SOUTHERN SPAIN: ALMERÍA, GRANADA, SEVILLA

While the artists and craftsmen of Cataluña looked forth to the world beyond their province for new ideas, those of southern Spain reflected on the glorious past when Al-Andalus of the Muslims was an important power. This retrospective attitude is quite apparent in the design of the green glassware blown at small furnaces in the region from the sixteenth to the nineteenth century. Most people living outside Spain remained unaware of the glasses produced in the provinces of Granada, Almería, Murcia and Jaén; and the Spaniards themselves, with eyes dulled by familiarity, regarded these objects as ordinary household goods of little interest. Not until the late nineteenth century did the realization occur to anyone that they might eventually prove valuable, and then it was the brothers Juan and Bonifacio Riaño who brought them to the attention of the art world. Now they are among the Spanish glasses most commonly found in museums and private collections everywhere.

During his travels back and forth through Spain, Bonifacio bought Spanish glasses, many of them Andalusian, until he owned well over three hundred. In 1873, a year after his death, his brother sold most of the collection to the Victoria and Albert Museum. For the entire group Juan Riaño drafted a preliminary catalogue, assigning objects to definite localities, such as Almería, Castril or Cartagena.[1] Although we do not know his reasons for the attributions, we may assume that his brother purchased each glass in the general vicinity of the city or town named as the original source.

In his book *The Industrial Arts in Spain,* first issued in 1879, Juan Riaño

[1] B. Riaño y Montero [List of glasses, 1873] Manuscript (B916) in the library of The Hispanic Society of America, New York.

acknowledged his indebtedness to Manuel Romero y Ortiz for notes on the southern glass centres.[1] This friend, who lived at Huéscar in Granada province, wrote down all the data that he had been able to collect about local factories.[2] Remains of fused and broken bits of glass (cullet) proved that a furnace existed at Pinar de la Vidriera, situated in the mountains between the provinces of Jaén and Granada and about fifteen miles from Puebla de Don Fadrique. A factory was operating there in 1620, according to a document in the town archives. At Castril de la Peña a glassworks owned by the Marchioness of Arenales was functioning in 1873. Since the building displayed an escutcheon of the Zafra family, who must have purchased it about 1492, the factory probably dated back to that time. Also indicative of its great antiquity was a mile-long shaft, on the outskirts of the town, where a special sand used in glassmaking was extracted from the earth.

Romero stated that a glass factory of ancient origin once existed at Arroyo de los Molinos, province of Jaén. About 1860, scarcity of fuel closed it down. From another source we learn that in 1850 the town had supported four glass factories, and that Bailén could boast of nine in which ordinary glass was produced.[3] Alcalá la Real, another town in the same province, manufactured glass of fine quality in the early sixteenth century, and Valdepeñas de Jaén had abundant fuel during the next two hundred years to run a furnace where excellent glass was blown.[4] In 1795, two more centres in Jaén province, Carolina and Hinojares, were making common glass.[5]

At María, province of Almería, several glasshouses formerly existed; one called 'del Campo' stood on the highway half a league from the city. Three factories functioned within the city limits, that belonging to the Botia family having been founded in 1750. Due to bad management on the owner's part, the establishment was abandoned forty years later. Shortly before it ceased to function, however, another was set up in the town by Antonio Triguero Serrano. This factory carried on the industry at María until 1854, when scarcity of wood to fire the furnaces brought production

---

[1] J. F. Riaño y Montero, *The Industrial Arts in Spain*, London, [1st edition] 1879, p. 231.

[2] M. Romero y Ortiz, Letter dated 30 September, 1873, Manuscript (B969) in the library of The Hispanic Society of America, New York.

[3] P. Madoz, *Diccionario geográfico-estadístico-histórico de España*, Madrid, 1850, vol. 3, pp. 31, 302.

[4] Gestoso y Pérez, *op. cit.* 1900, vol. 2, p. 401; B. Jiménez Patón, *Historia de la antigua y continuada nobleza de la ciudad de Iaē*, Jaén, 1628, *f* 9 [i.e. 14]; [J. Martínez de Mazas] *Retrato al natural de la ciudad y término de Jaén*, Jaén, 1794, p. 287.

[5] J. F. Riaño y Montero, *op. cit.*, 1879, p. 241.

to an end. Along the banks of the Almanzora River in Murcia province, a string of glass furnaces produced household objects. Until the mid-nineteenth century these glasses supplied the local markets.[1]

Glass vessels from the entire region have certain traits of colour, ornamentation and shape in common, whether they originated in Granada, Jaén or Almería. Colourless glass, known as crystal in Barcelona and Venice, was not made in the southern factories. Their metals, tinted green either accidentally by impurities in the silica or intentionally by the addition of iron oxides, ranged in shade from pale leaf-green to dark olive, from aquamarine to a rich emerald. Other minerals added to the pot gave brownish-black, purple, sapphire and cobalt-blues and amber-yellow. All the glass, whatever its colour, is filled with tiny air bubbles. Often in these Granadine glasses two colours are combined, the basic greens or amber-yellow being trimmed with emerald, black or sapphire. The neck of a blue-green vase (Plate 61) is decorated with a brownish-black wound thread, and its incrustation of handles and rings is similarly accented. A green mug (Plate 58) overlaid with dark purple glass looks as though it were full of wine. At Castril the glassmen attempted to correct the green coloration in the metal,[2] but a yellowish tonality persisted. They also blew the glass very thin. The objects attributed to María have thicker walls and more intense colours.

In 1871, the artist Mariano Fortuny wrote to a friend about a little glass vase which he had purchased at Granada, '. . . the form is purely Hispano-Arabic; the glass is greenish and thick.'[3] His words exactly describe a vast number of multi-handled vases from southern Spain, which show a remote but direct relationship with Syrian glass of the fourteenth century, especially with the mosque lamps. There are many variations on a basic theme wherein a conical neck seems more important than the sphere or piriform shape from which it emerges (Plates 47, 48A, 60). Rods or tubes forming the handles are attached to the collar and drawn down in ear-shaped curves that terminate in tips curled over or trailed down to the base. The Victoria and Albert Museum has a vase of this kind bristling with eight handles (Plate 46). Sometimes the glass-blower's enthusiasm resulted in fantastic loops (Plate 48B). Another example, blown in blue-green glass, seems based on a Persian shape, although it is unquestionably Spanish (Plate 62).

---

[1] Romero y Ortiz, MS (B969); M. Rico y Sinobas, *Del vidrio y sus artífices en España*, Madrid, 1873, p. 49.
[2] Gudiol Ricart and Artíñano, *op. cit.*, p. 68.
[3] J. C. Davillier, Baron, *Fortuny; sa vie, son œuvre, sa correspondance*, Paris, 1875, p. 70, *tr.*

# Southern Spain: Almería, Granada, Sevilla

Most of the vases are thick walled and heavily decorated with trailed threading, scallops, chains, pincered cresting and shell forms. Others of greater delicacy and more thinly blown show comparative restraint in their decoration. An example of pale yellow-green glass (Plate 48A), attributed to a factory at Castril, is thinly blown; the neck, octagonal in section, flares at the rim, around which winds emerald-green threading. Cords of yellow-green glass, trailed vertically and pinched together, form a net pattern round the spherical wall. Cockscomb crestings ornament the handles, and the ring foot is pincered into shape.

Flasks and small bottles are common shapes among the glasses of Granada and Almería (Plates 51B, 53A, 64A). They may be round, oval or pear-shaped, but all of them have small necks that could be corked or stoppered and walls flattened for easy carrying in a pocket or a saddlebag. Those attributed to Castril and other Granadine centres were blown from glass coloured in one of the several greens and were decorated with pinched serrations, shells and spiny projections trailed on in self-colour. María was probably the source of a sturdy flask (Colour plate B) of olive-green, its thick walls trailed with threading and a chain pattern.

A similar decoration on thickly blown emerald-green glass marks a drinking glass (Plate 64B) as having originated in the same locality. Like the flasks, its sides are flattened so that it might slip into a pocket. The Victoria and Albert and the British Museums have numerous examples of this shape, which is also well represented in the museums of Madrid and Granada. Some of these ellipsoidal glasses (Plate 64C), cobalt-blue as well as green, were blown in a mould that impressed upon them the words, 'Ave María'.

The drinking glasses produced in southern Spain range from wineglasses (Plate 51A) and mugs (Plate 58) to cups (Plate 57A). While they do not reach the high artistic standards of Catalan drinking glasses, a few of them, originating probably at Castril, compare favourably with Venetian-style work from other regions. Among these rare pieces may be numbered a goblet of thin, greenish glass (Plate 50), its faceted sides decorated simply with a trailed chain pattern, and a wineglass tinged faintly yellow (Plate 51A) with a thicket of pinched glass decoration round the stem.

Containers for wine, water and other liquids have numerous shapes, certain of them distinctly regional. A handsome jug of bubbly, green glass (Plate 63) shows an Islamic influence in its bulbous curves and the constriction at the middle. The graduated, looped threading that covers the entire surface was trailed on with unusual care. The shapes of two more jugs show how strong was the influence of metalwork on the glass-blowers. One (Plate 49A) of green glass covered by trailed threading, chains and a milled cord reproduces a silver ewer of the Renaissance, while the other (Plate 49B) presents the curving, fluted forms of an eighteenth-century silver vessel. Spouted containers, the porró for wine and the botijo for water (Plate 56), made of earthenware or glass, are typical of Spain, although they vary slightly in form from one province to another. The cruet for oil or vinegar is another spouted vessel. Sometimes blown from two gathers that were attached while still hot, the cruet takes on a double form (Plate 52) supplied with two spouts and one or more handles.

Glass was a material that Andalusians liked to use for oil lamps, and some of those made in southern Spain are not very different from the Catalan hanging lamps (Plate 36B) and table lamps (Plate 37) already described. A more usual shape in the south is the portable lamp from Castril with one or two spouts for the wicks and a large handle. An example in blue-green glass (Plate 54), resting on a stem and circular foot, shows the characteristic opening at the top, a folded and flared rim.

From the appearance of glasses manufactured during the late eighteenth century it is evident that the glass-blowers knew something about the work being done in Cataluña and Castilla. Although they attempted to decolorize the metal, the resulting glass was not completely colourless, but tinged faintly green or smoky yellow and blown rather thin. The shapes of certain pieces attributed to Castril look like direct copies of the two-handled, covered jars familiarly associated with the royal factory of La Granja de San Ildefonso. Vases (Plate 55) and footed bowls with wavy rims recall those made contemporaneously in Cataluña. A few of these bowls prove that glass-blowers of the south had learned at last a Venetian technique, known to the Catalans for more than two centuries, namely the methods for making frosted, or ice-glass.

Odd pieces for household purposes are a constant source of surprise among the assortment of Granadine glasses. As kitchen equipment there may be listed the linen smoothers (Plate 57B), perhaps for pleating starched ruffles, mortars with their accompanying pestles, and open salts (Plate 53A). Baskets, having sides built up from a moulded base with strands of glass pincered together (Plate 57D), seem to be purely ornamental but could have held sweetmeats. Cylindrical shakers with perforated tops comprised a part of the furniture of a writing desk, filled with sand for blotting wet ink. The purpose of a small bucket of yellow-green glass (Plate 57C) with a blue-green bulb inside is not easy to guess. As with the Catalans, the Granadine glass-blowers amused themselves in spare moments by creating small glass birds and animals of fantastic forms (Plate 53B).

Rather simple methods of shaping and working the glass are perceptible in the objects blown at the centres of Almería and Granada. The rims are cut off and melted smooth, with no further embellishment except to trail a thick thread round all bottle necks and so build up a flange for the edge. Bases are formed in several ways, the least complicated being the 'kick' or conical indentation pressed into the bottom of the object itself. An attached ring-foot supports many of the Andalusian glasses; for this type of base a small gather was worked to circular form and pinched into ripples like the edge of a piecrust (Plates 47, 48A–B). A conical foot (Plate 61) blown from a separate gather was often attached to the base, the paraison having been opened and the edge expanded and finished with a wide underfold. Or the attached bulb might be pressed flat to form a circular foot of double thickness. The glass-blower could also form such a foot by manipulating the vessel itself while it was still soft. This he did by rolling the blowpipe, with the bulb still attached, along the arms of his work bench, at the same time shaping up the foot with his tongs (Plates 56, 59).

Turning aside from the Andalusian provinces so prolific in their manufacture of glass, we come to the region of Sevilla and Córdoba, where a different history unfolds. After King Ferdinand III of Castilla reclaimed these territories from the Moors (1236–48), their people broke cultural ties with the remaining Islamic kingdoms to the east. No longer was artistic expression bound by the doctrine of Islam, as Christian influences swept in from northern Europe and Italy. With the beginning of the sixteenth century, a golden age dawned for Sevilla. Wealth and importance, gained through her position as principal seaport for trade with the Indies, attracted many foreigners to live within her gates. Among them were artists, craftsmen and traders who brought to shops and wharves a beautiful array of treasures – Flemish woven goods and pottery, German and Flemish metalwork and jewels, and the fragile glasses of Venice.

Throughout this period the Sevillian glassmen and vendors established their furnaces or salesrooms in the street called 'El Vidrio'. Many specialized in making stained glass for the windows of churches and the cathedral, but a few glass-blowers produced tableware and ornamental pieces. One of them, Juan Rodríguez, had come originally from Cadalso, the Castillian glass centre, whence he travelled to Venice and Barcelona. In both cities he worked for some years perfecting his art, before he settled at Sevilla. There he applied in 1557 for permission to set up a furnace. His sponsors, three glass-blowers and a merchant, testified that as a master craftsman he knew how to prepare green glass, *latticinio*-striped crystal glass of Venetian style and other favourite varieties.[1] The manufacture of glass continued at Sevilla throughout the sixteenth century and well into the next. The only other centre in the region seems to have been Cala, a town in Huelva province.

Among the glass-blowers who sailed from Sevilla for Mexico in the early days of colonization, there were probably a few Sevillians. Perhaps one or more of them joined ranks with those master craftsmen who in 1535 accompanied the first viceroy, Antonio de Mendoza, to New Spain. By 1542, the glass industry near Puebla de los Angeles had expanded remarkably. A report sent to the Emperor Charles called the industry unique in all New Spain. 'Three kinds of glass are blown and worked, crystal-white, green and blue, which supply Spaniards and natives of these regions as far as Guatemala and beyond, and the glasses even go to Peru and other countries.'[2]

In all probability the glasses of Sevilla resembled the wares of Barcelona and Venice, although no glass object has been classified with certainty as Sevillian. If such pieces exist, they have been attributed erroneously to other centres. The Sevillian artists Velázquez and Murillo painted glass vessels of considerable delicacy and beauty, perhaps locally blown yet conceivably Venetian or Italo-Flemish. Venetian-style glass may have been made at Cádiz by emigrés from Murano who settled there in the seventeenth century.[3]

Glass-blowing as a craft gave way to industrialization in the eighteenth century. Contemporary reports mention a flourishing industry at Sevilla, where many factories were operating, and record a single furnace at Cabra in southern Córdoba, where glass of an inferior quality was produced.[4] Foreign traders crowded into Spain to compete with native industries for the markets in the Spanish colonies of the New World. About 1730, Bohemian glass vendors opened permanent trading centres in port-cities, especially at Cádiz and Sevilla. The period of greatest prosperity for these traders was the last quarter of the eighteenth century when their storerooms were filled to capacity with valuable stock and their profits were most satisfactory. Often there were several German or Bohemian shops in one city, the total number in Spain having been computed as nearly one hundred

[1] Gestoso y Pérez, *op. cit.*, 1900, vol. 2, p. 401.
[2] M. R. de Terreros y Vinent, marqués de San Francisco, *Las artes industriales en la Nueva España*, Mexico, 1923, pp. 175–6, *tr.*
[3] Schuermans, *op. cit.*, 1890, p. 146.
[4] Espinalt, *op. cit.*, 1795, vol. 14, p. 34; J. F. Riaño y Montero, *op. cit.*, 1879, p. 241.

and fifty. The glasses sold from their showrooms to Spaniards or exported to the Americas included the engraved variety[1] and those enamelled in Central European style. The latter, found abundantly in Spain, are painted with simple designs in opaque white, brick-red, blue, yellow, green and black. Favourite decorations were flowers, song birds perched on hearts or boughs, men and women dressed in eighteenth-century costume. The escutcheons of Spain and Portugal, usually represented incorrectly, are frequently seen, combined with misspelled 'vivas' for Charles III and Charles IV, kings of Spain, and for John V of Portugal.

Most popular of these glasses so characteristic of Central Europe were the square or octagonal bottles with narrow necks threaded for screw tops or flanged for stoppers. Blown in moulds from blue, crystal or milk glass, they were used as liqueur bottles on sideboards or in travelling cases. Smaller versions were probably containers for perfume and toilet water from Cologne. Drinking glasses were of every kind, shaped for the consumption of numerous beverages: tumblers for water, mugs and tankards for beer and ale. Even to this day they may be purchased in the shops of Spanish dealers in antiques, where they are often attributed erroneously to Dutch glassmen who, it is claimed, operated furnaces in the regions of Valencia and Alicante.

While boxloads of Central European glass sailed to the Spanish colonies, other glasses also left the shores of Spain during the eighteenth century. From Cádiz and Sevilla went mirrors and glassware of France and Flanders, crystal glasses of England, beer and wine bottles of Bristol and Bayonne and the fine glass tableware made in the royal factory of La Granja de San Ildefonso.

---

[1] O. Quelle, *Die Faktoreien der sudetendeutschen Glashändler in Spanien und Portugal* (in *Ibero-amerikanisches Archiv*, October 1937, Jahr. 11, pp. 387–90); E. Dillon, *Glass*, London [1907] pp. 285–6.

# 4

## CASTILLA: CADALSO, RECUENCO, NUEVO BAZTÁN AND OTHER GLASS CENTRES OF THE REGION

By the early sixteenth century, Cadalso in the province of Madrid had become so noted for its glass products that it acquired popularly the name of Cadalso de los Vidrios, Cadalso 'of the Glasses'. Ferdinand and Isabel, the 'Catholic Kings', had at least one Cadalso glass, a drinking horn, among their table services in the Alcázar of Segovia. Their chaplain and historiographer, Marineo the Sicilian, observed in 1530 that the wares of Cadalso were far superior to the glasses produced at other Castillian towns. He remarked that Cadalso supplied the entire kingdom,[1] an indication that these glasses ranked high in quality.

As the century advanced, the inventories of prominent people, nobles and Philip II himself, continued to emphasize Cadalso as a glass centre of great importance, implying that its products, even though not so elegant as the Venetian and the Barcelonese, adequately served all domestic needs. Besides thirty ornate Venetian glasses, there belonged to Garcilaso de la Vega in 1536, the year of his death, 'more than a dozen glasses from Cadalso'.[2] In 1549, an inventory of goods belonging to Ana de Toledo, countess of Altamira, was filed at the city of Santiago. Among her many pieces of Venetian glass and Tuscan maiolica were listed 'more than twenty Cadalso glasses, including flasks'.[3] The third duke of Alburquerque left to his heirs in 1560 a wealth of foreign and domestic treasures, among them a

---

[1] Ferrandis Torres, *op. cit.*, vol. 3, p. 85; Marineo, *op. cit.*, $v^o f$ V.

[2] F. de San Román y Fernández, *ed., Documentos de Garcilaso, en el Archivo de protocolos de Toledo* (in R. Academia de la Historia, Madrid, *Boletín*, December 1918, vol. 73, p. 529, *tr.*).

[3] Academia Gallega, Coruña, *Colección de documentos históricos*, 1931, vol. 2, pp. 14–15, 16, *tr.*

goodly number of Venetian, German and Catalan glasses, and many blown at Cadalso. Aside from the water jugs, brandy 'kegs' and spouted cups in his pantry, the Duke had a decanter of blue glass with milk-white handles and a drinking glass with a blue handle, all from Cadalso.[1] Perhaps the workshops of other Castillian towns, if not Cadalso itself, supplied this nobleman with numerous utility glasses, the sources of which are not mentioned in the inventory. For El Pardo Palace in 1564, Philip II chose the decorative glasses of Venice and Barcelona to sparkle with gilt and crystal on the royal dinner table, but the domestic equipment for this palace included glasses of Cadalso – seventeen lamps, sixteen urinals and half-a-dozen flasks.[2]

Glasses found within the Castillian region have sometimes been attributed to the Cadalso factories without sufficient reason. So it was with two wineglasses existing in a monastery near Cadalso for over three centuries.[3] In claiming a Castillian origin for them, the Spanish scholars have overlooked the possibility that the glasses may have been imported from Venice about 1548, when Spain was such a good market for Venetian crystal that the sale of Cadalso ware decreased alarmingly.[4] In shape, both of the wineglasses are distinctly Venetian, and the *millefiori* bowl of one glass points rather convincingly to Venice. The simplified pattern of enamels and gilding on the other, which has a crystal bowl and a blue stem and foot, indicates that it may have been blown and decorated somewhere outside Italy, by an artisan who had emigrated from his native land.[5]

How many glass factories existed at Cadalso during the sixteenth century we have yet to learn. The name of only one glass-blower has emerged from historical records, that of Juan Rodríguez who left his native town to work and study elsewhere (see pp. 57–58). All indications are that several furnaces were kept busy with a brisk trade. By 1645, three furnaces were in operation, run under the patronage of the Marquis of Villena. The glasses produced there, comparable with the Venetian, were of the finest quality, of beautiful colours and graceful shapes.[6] One of the establishments closed down a few years later, but it was revived in 1692 by an industrialist who also had charge of the glassworks at San Martín de Valdeiglesias. This re-established factory produced not only hollow ware but also window-panes to be sold throughout the province of Madrid.

---

[1] *Inventario . . . del . . . tercer duque de Alburquerque*, pp. 101–2.
[2] Sánchez Cantón, *op. cit.*, pp. 73–5.
[3] Illustrated in Frothingham, *Barcelona Glass*, figs. 5–6; J. F. Riaño y Montero, *op. cit.*, 1890, p. 238.
[4] M. Colmeiro, *Historia de la economía política en España* [Madrid, 1863] vol. 2, p. 326, note 2.
[5] Frothingham, *Barcelona Glass*, p. 15.
[6] R. Mendes Silva, *Poblacion general de España*, Madrid, 1645, *f* 40.

## Castilla: Cadalso, Recuenco, Nuevo Baztán

Between 1600 and 1606, Valladolid was the capital of Spain, and there Thomé Pinheiro da Veiga noted the pomp and festivities of the court of Philip III. The observations of this Portuguese scholar resulted from a careful study of manners and customs gained during the two or three years that he lived among Spanish grandees. Nothing was too minute for his comment, and he lingered over descriptions of every luxury of food, drink and clothing. The glassware sold at six shops in Valladolid delighted him with its beauty. 'Glasses of the greatest size . . . of all shapes and colours, and others . . . for distilling water . . . retorts, and a thousand inventions, which here [at Lisbon] we never see, are not very expensive.'[1] Although Veiga thought that these glasses were made at Valladolid, they came more probably from Cadalso or other Castillian centres, or perhaps from Cataluña, transported on muleback in straw-filled panniers and brought either directly to the city or via the Medina del Campo fairs.

Within the same terrain as Cadalso, mountainous and rich in forests that could supply wood for firing and in deposits of refractory clays for crucibles, a number of glass factories flourished. At Cebreros, crystal glass was being made during the first years of the seventeenth century. The director of the concern wrote to Count Gondomar, who later became ambassador from Spain to the Court of James I of England, to announce that the first crystal had just been produced at the Cebreros factory. He was sending to Valladolid a basket of these glasses for the Countess.[2]

This century was a time when Italian and Flemish glassworkers flocked to Spain, many of them settling in Castilla. In 1608, a furnace was constructed at El Escorial through the combined efforts of a Ragusan merchant, who supplied the capital, and the Venetian glass-blower, Domingo Barovier, who supervised production. The latter, member of a prominent family of Murano, had come more recently from Palma de Mallorca (see p. 34). Typical of the itinerant glassmen was Antonio Pellizari, a Venetian who wandered to Flanders, where he worked for a while. He then persuaded two Flemish artisans to journey with him to Madrid, and by July of 1678 they had built a glass furnace within the grounds of the Royal Palace to make mirrors and window-panes of fine crystal. A few months later Pellizari ran into trouble and fled to Portugal, where he established himself at Lisbon.[3]

Another factory directed by an Italo-Fleming, Guglielmo Toreata,

---

[1] T. Pinheiro da Veiga, *Pincigraphia ou descripção e historia natural e moral de Valhadolid* (in his *Fastigimia*, Porto, 1911, pp. 339–40, *tr*).

[2] Schuermans (*op. cit.*, 1890, p. 145) gives the date of the letter as 1606, and in J. F. Riaño (*op. cit.*, 1890, p. 240) the date is printed as 1690. Since the Count lived only until 1626, obviously the latter is incorrect.

[3] Schuermans, *op. cit.*, 1890, pp. 141–2, 166.

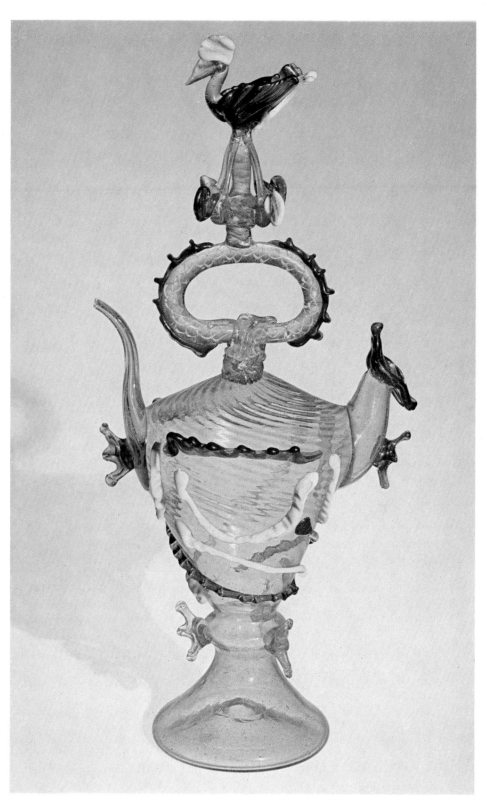

C. *Càntir, with blue and white trailed threading and pincered decorations.*
*Cataluña, eighteenth century. Ht.* 16$\frac{1}{16}$ *in. (40.8 cm.)*
*The Corning Museum of Glass, Corning (New York)*
(*See page* 49)

opened in 1689 somewhere in Castilla la Nueva, a region comprising the provinces of Madrid, Toledo, Guadalajara, Cuenca and Ciudad Real. After ten years, the factory was still in operation under the supervision of an Italian master, Giacomo Bertoletti.[1] Could Guglielmo Toreata be the same as the Guillermo Torcada who experimented in 1692 at Torre de Esteban Hambrán in Toledo province? The similarities of name, time and place indicate this possibility. The eighteenth-century author who referred to this furnace may have given Toreata's name in the Castillian form or in a misspelled version, even as he misspelled the name of the village by writing 'Hambroz' for 'Hambrán'. Torcada's (or Toreata's) work there resulted in failure after four months' time. The glass that he made, although of fine quality, cracked too easily. A Catalan blower, called in to continue production at the factory, was unable to please the Castillian customers.[2]

From the Low Countries in 1680 came Dieudonné Lambotte, glass-blower of Namur. He and his brothers had closed down the window-pane and mirror factory inherited from their father, Thierry Lambotte, and Dieudonné under the sponsorship of the Spanish governor of Flanders started forth to Madrid, taking with him Flemish equipment and enough workers to open a new factory. Soon he left Madrid for San Martín de Valdeiglesias, near Cadalso, a more suitable locality for his glassworks. Until his death three years later, Lambotte and his company of Flemings produced Venetian-style crystal. His Italian successor, although skilled in constructing furnaces and mixing pot-metals, knew too little about blowing and shaping glasses, and the imperfect products that resulted failed to sell at the company's shop in Madrid. Attempts by the director of a Cadalso factory to revive the Lambotte works about 1692 ended unsuccessfully.[3]

The wanderings of glassmen between Spanish-controlled Flanders and Spain were not always directed from the northern country to the southern. Recorded as having migrated to Brussels was the Spaniard, Francisco del Bueno. Perhaps a promoter of the industry rather than a true glassworker, he wished to maintain a factory for making Venetian-style crystals. In 1623, he came into conflict with Antonio Miotti, an Italo-Fleming, who previously had been granted exclusive rights for the manufacture of such glass.[4]

The revival of furnaces at Valdemaqueda, a town between El Escorial and San Martín de Valdeiglesias, has been accredited to Juan Danis and

[1] Schuermans, *op. cit.*, 1890, p. 142.

[2] E. Larruga y Boneta, *Memorias políticas y económicas sobre los frutos, comercio, fábricas y minas de España*, Madrid, 1792, vol. 16, pp. 222–3.

[3] R. Chambon, *L'histoire de la verrerie en Belgique*, Brussels, 1955, pp. 112, 114–15; Schuermans, *op. cit.*, 1890, pp. 142–3; Larruga, *op. cit.*, vol. 16, pp. 222–3.

[4] Schuermans, *op. cit.*, 1889, pp. 218–20.

Francisco Herranz from Segovia. About 1676, they acquired a glass factory, long idle, that dated back to the previous century. Their original plan was to make coloured glasses for the windows of Segovia Cathedral; but experimentation led Danis on to producing blown-glass vessels of many shapes, while Herranz concentrated on the stained-glass windows.

Their processes of manufacture Danis carefully noted, writing down the names of local barillas, refractory clays and silicas. Many of the formulae and techniques that he recorded were based on Antonio Neri's famous treatise, *L'Arte vetraria*, which, translated and published in numerous editions, was widely read by master glassmen everywhere. The strongest barilla, wrote the Spaniard, was from Cieza near Cartagena, while those with the least discoloration came from the marshes around Murcia and the region of Alicante. Black clay found in a gully that lay between San Martín de Valdeiglesias and Cadalso was combined with a white clay of Segovia to make the crucibles and the hoods of furnaces. The iron tools listed as necessary to the Valdemaqueda furnace were all required in the processes of blowing and manipulating glass. Drawings of these furnaces, crucibles and tools appeared on the margins of Danis's text.[1]

The mixtures for crystal presented difficulties, for they tended toward instability; yet they were supposedly the same as those used in France and Flanders and at San Martín de Valdeiglesias. The finished glasses of Valdemaqueda deteriorated if filled with vinegar or left in a damp atmosphere. This fault must have been corrected eventually, since in 1680 Valdemaqueda glasses were considered replicas of the Venetian, selling for as much as those of Barcelona.[2]

Far more is known about the history of glassmaking in Madrid province than about the appearance of products from its furnaces. Piecing together the rare descriptions from contemporary sources, we can say with reason that the glasses from most of these workshops were blown in imitation of the Venetian. Also, they resembled Italo-Flemish and Catalan glasses enough to confuse the original buyers. After the passage of centuries, it is even more difficult to distinguish Castillian glasses from others. Since Cadalso's factories, active over a long span of time, were most famous of all, a number of glasses have been attributed to this town, especially if they were found in the vicinity. By the late sixteenth century, the workers at Cadalso and El Escorial apparently knew the Venetian method for making

[1] The manuscript for the treatise existed until 1802 in the archives of Segovia Cathedral, but it has since disappeared. (I. Bosarte, *Viage artístico á varios pueblos de España*, Madrid, 1804, vol. 1, pp. 93–5; Pérez Bueno, *Vidrios y vidrieras*, pp. 111–13.)

[2] Segovia (City). Ordinances, etc. *Tassa general y moderación de precios de todos generos de mantenimientos*, Madrid, 1680, p. 28.

*latticinio*-striped glass, a process learned through Venetian and Catalan glass-blowers who journeyed to Castilla.

The striped, feathered and braided decorations on glasses attributed to the Castillian factories show irregularities, an uncertainty in execution or a coarseness of detail that sets them apart from Catalan or Venetian models. The clear glass meant for crystal is lightly tinged with green or smoky yellow; minute bubbles and unfused impurities give it a turbid look. Uneven streaks of violet sometimes mar the crystal, a discoloration due to excessive manganese. Some of these defects show up in a bowl (Plate 65B) with milk-white feathering and blue rim, handles and base. The technique differs from the conventional Venetian method in which canes of *latticinio* were embedded in a gather of clear glass and then blown. In making this bowl the glass-blower trailed threads of white on the surface and then dragged through them with a pointed tool. A cup (Plate 65A) of brilliantly clear, smoky yellow, differing in quality from Catalan glass, may have come from a Cadalso factory. The chain pattern trailed round the bowl and the pincered cresting, like a cockscomb, along the handle are in the Venetian manner. The shape bears a certain resemblance to Flemish glasses of the late sixteenth century, an indication perhaps that it was blown by an Italo-Fleming who worked in Castilla.

The heavy forms of the early seventeenth century, primarily goblets and flower vases, have handles and other decorative additions that failed to reproduce the airy fragility of Venetian work. In two-handled vases of bubbly, pale green glass (Plates 66, 73) this coarseness is quite apparent. The striped piece was shaped from a single gather, making a double thickness for the base. The collar is uneven, and the handles with their dark blue cresting are far from symmetrical. The wide, uneven stripes running down the pear-shaped bulge are the result of blue-white threads trailed on the surface of a partially expanded bulb and marvered, followed by further blowing. The pear-shaped vase, undecorated except for the handles, has a sturdy, pedestal base blown from a separate gather.

*Latticinio* stripes trail diagonally across a goblet of clear, greenish glass (Plate 67) with a rim tooled into octagonal shape. To ornament this goblet the glassworker drew cords of blue glass between the bowl and the knop and applied two handles, pulling and pinching them flat to resemble butterfly wings. The pattern of *latticinio* braid that decorates a slender vase (Plate 68) seems to have been achieved by the Venetian and Catalan method of embedding canes of twisted *latticinio* into a mass of clear metal dropped into a mould. This molten material was expanded by blowing, and in the case of this piece, the bubble was twisted and worked with tools to form the collar. Fantastic handles were made by building up one rod of glass on another, crimping them with saw-toothed crests or flattening them with pincers that pressed a crisscross pattern on the surfaces. Another Castillian piece is a vase (Plate 69) of greenish glass marred by a profusion of bubbles. The ear-shaped handles are topped with blue glass pinched into spines, and the rim is threaded with *latticinio*. A broad band consisting of a white stripe between two of purple glass encircles the vase, the coloured bands having been pulled across the molten surface of the vase and twisted into swirls by the callipers. This manipulation of the glass shows originality but the workmanship lacks perfection, and the resulting form tends to be cumbersome.

During the last years of the seventeenth century, the glass industry in the region near Madrid fell into a steady decline and even failed completely at a number of centres. Glasses blown and decorated 'à la façon de Venise' were no longer in demand, because suddenly it was modish to admire the styles fashionable in France, brought to the nation's capital in 1700 by Philip V. The choicest glass came to mean crystal that was wheel-engraved and gilded. As Spanish factories were unable to supply this type of glass, all of it for some years had to be imported. Spaniards strove to keep their furnaces operating or they opened new factories in an attempt to furnish the luxury crystals popular with the noblemen of Madrid.

Fortunately for a few glassmen, they received state protection, special grants and subsidies to further their efforts. Even so, they did not always succeed. In 1720, Juan de Goyeneche built a glass factory at a site near Madrid and Alcalá de Henares, naming it Nuevo Baztán after his native town in Navarra. From Philip V he obtained a grant for the new factory and its workers, assuring them of royal protection, liberal tax exemptions and other favours. Goyeneche and his heirs were given permission to maintain for thirty years as many furnaces as necessary to make mirrors, window-panes and hollow ware. The royal grant prohibited the importation of foreign crystals to Castilla and limited the number of aliens working at Nuevo Baztán to those who were instructing Spanish artisans in the manufacture of crystal glass and in the art of wheel-engraving. This method of decorating glass was new to Spaniards, so that in this phase of the industry they turned to foreigners for help.

Goyeneche gathered together about twenty families of foreign glass-blowers who had been employed by two promoters, Tomás del Burgo and Jean-Baptiste de la Pomeraye from Saint-Gobain, France, whose ventures in crystal manufacture failed in 1712 and 1718. For these destitute aliens and for the Spaniards joining them he built furnaces and ample workrooms, supplied all necessary materials and tools and supported the glassworkers at his own expense. Their living quarters and his own palace were designed by the famous architect, Churriguera. The materials used in building the factory and for its equipment were the best obtainable, the refractory clay for furnaces and crucibles having been transported many miles on muleback from Tortosa in Cataluña. Although this costly clay was resistant to high temperatures, the furnaces twice crumbled during the initial firings. Still hopeful, Goyeneche disregarded all entreaties to abandon the enterprise, and his determination to succeed was rewarded after the third trial.

Soon the Nuevo Baztán factory was supplying Madrid and other parts of Spain with engraved crystals. Some of them travelled as far as the Spanish colonies in America. Mindful of the royal protection gained for his factory, Goyeneche ordered tableware to be made for the royal house, including a dinner set for Queen Isabel Farnese. A single tumbler from this service is now in the Royal Palace at Madrid (Plate 75B). Cut in a ring round the vase is a series of fleurs-de-lis, above which appears the wheel-engraved escutcheon of Philip V. A crown surmounts the shield, which is supported by a cherub, and the Order of the Golden Fleece encircles it. A crizzling, perhaps caused by faulty annealing, marks the tumbler as the product of a factory still beset by trials.

Because the law governing importation of crystals had not been enforced, the products of Nuevo Baztán were greatly undersold by the vendors of foreign goods. This pressure decided Goyeneche to establish a salesroom in his Madrid home on the Calle de Alcalá, a palace that now houses the Real Academia de Bellas Artes de San Fernando. An Englishman arriving at the factory shortly after 1720 proposed a plan to manufacture English-style crystal. Goyeneche accepted unhesitatingly the offer of this man to finance the construction of a special furnace where he eventually made many experiments. Unfortunately the project came to nothing, since a clear glass of the desired brilliance failed to develop.

Dwindling fuel supplies at last forced Goyeneche to move his factory to a more wooded spot, the new location being Villanueva de Alcorón in the Cuenca mountains. Wood for firing was more abundant there, but the quality of the raw materials seemed to affect the glass mixtures. Pot-metals that formerly produced crystal now gave an ordinary glass, like that made at nearby Recuenco. Production at the Nuevo Baztán factory ceased about 1728, and the workers returned to their native lands or scattered to other parts of Spain.[1]

---

[1] Artiñano, *La fabricación de vidrios en el Nuevo Baztán* (in *Arte español*, Madrid, 1929, vol. 10, pp. 427–9; Larruga, *op. cit.*, 1791, vol. 10, pp. 54–63).

## Castilla: Cadalso, Recuenco, Nuevo Baztán

No haphazard chance led Goyeneche to choose Villanueva de Alcorón as the new site for his factory. Several small towns and villages clustering together where Guadalajara and Cuenca provinces meet were active centres of glass manufacture, and undoubtedly the industrialist moved into the same locality hoping to enjoy the advantages of inexpensive local materials. Arbeteta and Beteta produced bottles, decanters and mugs of ordinary glass for household purposes, and tradition in the eighteenth century had it that the furnaces of Recuenco, Armallones and Vindel had been operating for years.

References to Cuenca glass date back as far as 1599, when Diego Fernández de Córdoba, a knight-commander of Calatrava, died and left to his heirs eighty Cuenca glasses, along with forty-four Venetian glasses and two hundred and six from Barcelona.[1] In 1628 a designer of stained-glass windows for Burgos Cathedral was told by the chapter to buy glass from the factory at Cuenca for constructing his windows.[2] A contemporary description of Cuenca city refers to more than one glass furnace in operation there.[3] In 1680, the prices for Recuenco, Beteta and Cuenca glasses were considered reasonable as compared with prices for French imports and Valdemaqueda glasses in Venetian style.[4]

There is little basis for associating certain glasses with the Guadalajara-Cuenca region. The theory that a small group of vases in the Macaya collection, Barcelona, came from the furnaces at Recuenco rests principally on the fact that they all were found in a house at Cuenca.[5] If these vases were, indeed, products of the Recuenco factories, then the same provenance may be given to others possessing identical qualities. Recognizable in them is the Venetian style of glass-blowing – a free-blown technique, eggshell thinness of the walls, together with pinched and threaded decorations. Yet in shape they are quite distinctly a related group, set apart from the glasses of Venice, Cataluña and southern Spain.

The most common form (Plate 70) is footed, the body a small sphere upon which is set a cone-shaped collar with the rim worked to octagonal shape. The quality of the glass indicates that these objects emerged at a time of experimentation. The results, not always satisfactory, were glasses cloudy with bubbles and tinged green or amber. At times, one finds a piece with all brilliance gone because the surface is pitted by minute erosions. A

---

[1] Pérez Pastor, *op. cit.*, 1910, vol. I, p. 314.
[2] Rico y Sinobas, *op. cit.*, p. 48.
[3] L. Sánchez Costa, *La península á principios del siglo XVII* (in *Revue hispanique*, Paris, 1915, vol. 34, pp. 354–8).
[4] Segovia (City). Ordinances, etc. pp. 12, 17.
[5] Information given verbally by José Gudiol Ricart.

strange dampness collects on the surface, to form minute crystals, an unstable and destructive condition that is known as 'glass disease'. Such decomposition, if not properly treated, progresses and the object, unless kept in an extremely dry atmosphere, would in time disintegrate completely. This irreversible form of decay has affected the bell-shaped vase of Plate 75A. This piece, of pale amber streaked with blue, has ring-handles and threading of sapphire blue. The spiral ribbing and the octagonal shape of the rim are seen in several vases of this type; a greenish vase (Plate 71) threaded with milk-white has the same characteristics. Ribbing swirls diagonally round a thistle-shaped goblet-vase of greenish brown glass (Plate 72). The bowl is held high on a hollow knopped stem and a domed foot. Loop-handles on opposite sides of the vase are each decorated with a trailed cord pinched into a serrated edge, and threads of glass encircle the rim and the foot. The same sort of decoration ornaments the handles of a sturdy vase (Plate 74) blown from green glass that is streaked with purplish brown.

When Fernando López de Aragón built a glass furnace at Recuenco in 1722, there were already three others in operation. Later, Diego Dorado purchased this factory, which he and his family continued to operate until the end of the century. Dorado was well aware of Philip V's policy of state protection for industries, following the principles of the French economist, Colbert. Thus encouraged, the industrialist appealed in 1734 to the King for special grants, exemptions from taxes and duties and freedom from military service for the glass-blowers. Since the factory was to supply the palace with storage bottles for wine and water and with drug jars for the King's pharmacy, Dorado asked that the royal arms might be displayed over the entrance door of the factory. He sought permission also to cut an unlimited amount of wood from the oak and pine groves belonging to the crown. This petition Philip denied, although in 1740 he permitted Dorado certain privileges, among them the right to run a salesroom at Madrid. Equal rights were given to the two other glass factories still in operation at Recuenco, and these privileges continued for the next ten years.

For the periods of time when Recuenco glass was selling in Madrid, the carters bringing it to the capital stayed at an inn called 'La Gallega'. To prove that their wares were authentic products of the Dorado factory, they carried with them affidavits signed by the mayor of Recuenco. The glasses themselves could not be marked because the material was too delicate.[1]

Any grants withheld from the Dorado factory by Philip V were conceded

---

[1] Larruga, *op. cit.*, 1792, vol. 19, p. 261.

eventually by Charles III, whose policy was to put Spanish factories on a sound financial basis by offering them state guardianship. The Dorado grandsons, Diego and Joaquín Ruiz Dorado, who had inherited the factory in 1787, presented their case to the King, requesting his protection in return for supplies of Recuenco glasses for the palace wine cellar. They proudly called attention to the improved condition of their factory with its enlarged buildings, to its usefulness in the community on account of its employing so many workmen and to the glasses that showed such careful workmanship. Their finest glass, which they sent to Court in the form of bottles and window-panes, found a ready market all over Spain and in Portugal. These reports that the Dorado factory made glass pharmacy jars for the King encourage us to consider certain bottles and covered jars originally in the Madrid Palace pharmacy, as being Recuenco glasses. It is very possible, too, that Recuenco furnished the eighteenth-century pharmacy in the Hospital of San Juan Bautista at Toledo. Still to be seen on the shelves, mixed in with albarellos of Talavera pottery, are numerous glass retorts, bottles and flasks.

Stimulated by the willingness of Charles III to help them, the Dorados planned in 1788 to open a factory for the production of crystals of several grades. At this period Germans had the reputation for surpassing all others in the manufacture of crystal glass, and since foreigners were then welcome in Spain, the brothers employed a group of Germans to start the new project. Experimenting with local materials, they built a furnace and the crucibles for melting glass mixtures. Soon, with tools and machines brought from their homeland they started to make glasses that showed great skill and beauty. The Dorados gave the King their vases, cruets, salt-cellars and many other objects in the hope of impressing him with the foreigners' work.

After six months, the brothers petitioned King Charles to support this factory by extending to it the same privileges given formerly to their other factories. Production of German-style crystal had proved costly, so that they were no longer able to finance the venture. They sought enough capital to retain the German artisans who made these excellent crystals and were teaching the entire operation to six young apprentices. While King Charles granted their petitions in 1789, the money, their most urgent need, was not forthcoming, and the lack of it brought the Recuenco scheme to an end.[1] The industry, although it deteriorated greatly, continued on until the middle of the nineteenth century, the last two factories producing sheet glass and hollow ware. Until the end, the glasses were pronounced the most

[1] Larruga, *op. cit.*, 1792, vol. 19, pp. 260–87.

beautiful and crystal-clear of any made in Spain.[1] While the Dorado crystal factory was in full swing, the furnace at Vindel, a town near by, for years manufactured ordinary glass. Toward the end of the eighteenth century, however, many of its workmen left to join the Recuenco factories.[2]

Simultaneously, the three factories that had managed to survive at Cadalso became reduced to two, both the property of the Marchioness of Villena. A contemporary writer reported, 'A furnace has been lost, and also the fame that its glasses had for clarity and variety throughout Castilla.'[3] During the nineteenth century, two factories produced 'all kinds of vessels which compete with the best in the kingdom'.[4] A family by the name of Sáez became proprietors of one of the factories at Cadalso, and this they handed down from generation to generation. Their products, no longer the decorative objects of the past, were restricted to decanters, lamp chimneys and bottles of greenish glass. Old methods of production were retained to a degree, notably the furnaces fired with wood; because of this antiquated equipment, certain traditions lingered on among the workmen, fostered with patriarchal beneficence by the proprietors. After the wood had been gathered each year and stored, the entire town celebrated, feasting on roast lamb and wine supplied by the Sáez family. Another festival, partly religious, marked the lighting of the furnace. The workmen, dressed in gala costume, gathered at the village church and lighted tapers from the vigil candles. Walking in solemn procession, they bore the fire to the glass factory, where they started the furnace burning to the accompaniment of prayers and the priest's blessing.[5]

[1] Madoz, *op. cit.*, 1849, vol. 13, p. 390; A. L. J. Laborde, comte de, *Itinéraire descriptif de l'Espagne*, Paris, 1827–9, vol. 1, p. 383; vol. 5, p. 361.
[2] Larruga, *op. cit.*, 1792, vol. 19, pp. 287–91.
[3] Larruga, *op. cit.*, 1791, vol. 10, pp. 53–4.
[4] Madoz, *op. cit.*, 1849, vol. 5, p. 111, *tr.*
[5] Notes by Andrés Francesch (in Planell, *op. cit.*, vol. 2, pp. 103–[108]).

# 5

## THE ROYAL FACTORY OF
## LA GRANJA DE SAN ILDEFONSO

A Catalan glassworker, Ventura Sit, left the Nuevo Baztán factory in 1728 to build a glass furnace at San Ildefonso, near the palace of La Granja. For the next eight years he blew small panes of muff glass for windows and mirrors. Impressed with his labours, the queen, Isabel Farnese, had a factory built for him within the royal estate, where he and other trained artisans from Castilla and Cataluña might work for the royal residences. King Philip V became interested in the experiments and urged Sit to manufacture larger plates of glass for palace mirrors. Soon another Catalan workman, Pedro Fronvila, invented a machine for pouring the molten glass on a brass table and polishing it with seventeen wooden polishers.

Examples of small mirrors believed to have been produced by Sit, Fronvila and their companions may be seen at Madrid in the Museo Arqueológico Nacional as part of the former Rico y Sinobas collection. Their surfaces are wheel-engraved with scenes of huntsmen, Biblical parables and the *Seasons*. The engraving on these mirrors and on a group of drinking glasses from the same collection is so Germanic that their Spanish origin is questionable, even though this type of work was done at the San Ildefonso factory during the early years of its existence.

Until 1755 Ventura Sit served as supervisor over the manufacture of plate glass. His salary, twenty-eight reales daily, was well above the sums given to other employees, an indication that the King appreciated his work. After Sit's death that year, his widow petitioned for a more substantial pension, reminding the King that her husband had taught almost all the master craftsmen then working at the factory.[1]

[1] Pérez Bueno, *Real fábrica de cristales de San Ildefonso (La Granja); antecedentes y apuntes para su historia* (in *Arte español.*, Madrid, 1926, vol. 8, p. 12).

## The Royal Factory of La Granja de San Ildefonso

Contemporary accounts of San Ildefonso mirrors are unanimous in describing them as the largest produced anywhere in Europe. The casting, rolling, grinding and polishing of the glass plates was described in 1755 by an Italian who visited the factory: 'The process of pouring them is altogether ingenious. From the large furnace they draw a clay crucible containing molten crystal and pour it on a great brass frame that has been heated red-hot. Carried to the edge of the frame by a machine to which it is held by four iron chains, the crucible is tipped skilfully and all the crystal, which is of a thin consistency, spreads and begins to harden. Then it is drawn into a little oven at the end of the table and left there as long as necessary to anneal.'[1] The glass was then ready for grinding and polishing.

As time went on, larger and larger frames were constructed, so that plates of glass could be made to measure over thirteen feet high and almost eight feet wide. During the reign of Ferdinand VII (1814–33), there was found in a storage room of the factory a mirror so large that a mounted horseman could have seen his reflection in it.[2]

Twice during the existence of Sit's factory the building caught fire, destroying the major part of the workrooms. Charles III (1759–88), mindful of the situation, ordered a group of court architects to design and build a new factory, placing it for safety's sake outside the boundary walls of the royal estate, but near the palace grounds. These men, hoping to surpass the best glass factories of Europe, constructed a palatial edifice having two great furnaces covered by high cupolas to enclose the smoke vents. Between the towers ran a single-storeyed structure containing offices, living quarters for the workmen, storerooms for supplies and galleries for every process of glass manufacture. A pen-and-ink sketch of the building was drawn by the Spanish artist Francisco Van Halen, probably in the mid-nineteenth century.[3]

Many localities in Spain furnished the royal factory with necessary raw materials. Fuel for the furnaces came from the forests near by, and the white sands of Lastras de Cuéllar and Bernui were but a few leagues distant in upper Segovia province. Barilla was carried on muleback along the tiresome journey from localities in Murcia province; refractory clay for furnaces and crucibles was transported from a site near Horta, in Tarragona

---

[1] [N. Caimo] *Voyage d'Espagne, fait en l'année 1755*, Paris, 1772, pt. 2, pp. 59 [i.e. 49]–50, *tr*. The Royal Factory apparently switched to plate-glass about 1736 (Pérez Bueno, *Vidrio* (in *Folklore y costumbres de España*, edited by F. Carreras y Candi, Barcelona, 1931, vol. 2, p. [513]).
[2] S. M. Sedeño, *Descripción del real sitio de San Ildefonso*, Segovia, 1867, p. 41.
[3] Illustrated in Pérez Bueno, *Vidrios y vidrieras*, opposite p. 128.

province; while zaffre was brought from the Pyrenees and manganese for decolorizing was procured from Alcañiz in Aragón.

The division for plate glass manufacture at San Ildefonso next came under the supervision of an Irish engineer named John Dowling, who invented a polishing machine that worked by hydraulic power. Although much hand labour was thus eliminated, the manager of the royal factory reported in 1764 that in his opinion this machine afforded no economy whatsoever.[1] Dowling was still in charge of the polishing machine when an English traveller visited the factory in 1772 and wrote: 'I called on Mr. John Dowling, an Irishman . . . This gentleman was so kind as to accompany me during my stay here. We first visited the royal fabric for plate glass . . . These plates are not made for sale, but only for the king's use. . . . Mr. Dowling has likewise erected a machine which polishes forty-eight plates of glass at a time.'[2]

For some unknown reason, in 1783, Dowling was thrown into prison, and we hear no more of him. He left the mirror factory in a thriving condition, equipped with three bronze tables of graduated sizes. On these frames the molten glass was poured and a cylinder was rolled over it to extend and flatten the mass. Necessary to the process were twenty annealing ovens 'into which the glasses, still red-hot, are conveyed, where they remain hermetically enclosed for the space of fifteen to twenty-five days, until they gradually cool. All those that are cracked, or have any imperfections, are cut for hand mirrors, window-panes, or glasses for carriages . . . .'[3]

The next phase of the work on plate glass was the grinding, done by a manual operation, which consisted in rubbing one against another, putting between them water and sand, more or less fine, according to the progress of the operation. The upper plate of glass, which is in a state of perpetual motion, while that underneath remains immovable, is much sooner ground, so that five of the former are reduced to the required thickness before one of the lower glasses. This is a laborious and monotonous process, for one single glass frequently occupies one workman for more than two months.

'When they are sufficiently ground on both sides, they are polished in the following manner: if they are of the greatest size, this operation is performed by hand in the same workshop. Those of middle size are conveyed to a machine, in which thirty polishers are set in motion by water. They are

[1] Pérez Bueno, *Real fabrica*, p. 13.
[2] R. Twiss, *Travels through Portugal and Spain, in 1772 and 1773*, London, 1775, p. 87.
[3] [J. M. J. Fleuriot, marquis de Langle] *Voyage en Espagne* [n.p.] 1785, vol. I, pp. 26–7; Jean François, baron de Bourgoing, *Tableau de l'Espagne moderne*, 2nd edition, Paris, 1797, vol. I, p. 199, *tr.*

square boxes, each containing inside it a plate of lead. Placed perpendicularly over the glass and covered underneath with a smooth felt, they are pushed in a horizontal direction by a wooden handle attached to them. The glass is first rubbed by hand with emery supplied by a quarry in the vicinity of Toledo. . . . After this process, the glass is covered with a reddish earth, called "almagro", and placed under the polishing machine. This procedure must be followed on both sides of the glass and lasts eight or ten days.

'An experiment was made to introduce mechanical power as a substitute for manual labour in grinding the glass. For this purpose machines were brought from France to San Ildefonso, but the directors of the establishment, having seen that this more costly method was not much more expeditious than the old one, abandoned it altogether. The glasses thus ground and polished are conveyed finally to Madrid to be quicksilvered' [for mirrors].[1]

In 1786, an Englishman said of the San Ildefonso mirror factory: 'The glass manufacture is here carried to a degree of perfection unknown in England. The largest mirrors . . . are designed wholly for the royal palaces, and for presents from the king. Yet, even for such purposes it is ill placed, and proves a devouring monster in a country where provisions are dear, fewel scarce, and carriage exceedingly expensive.'[2]

Orders to supply mirrors for the King's residences kept the glassworkers busy over a long period at the royal factory. During the decade between 1763 and 1774, Charles III commissioned wall mirrors and crystal chandeliers, many of which remain today in their original positions. To mention only a few, the great throne room in the Madrid Palace and the two porcelain rooms, one at Madrid and the other at Aranjuez, were hung with these tall mirrors set in frames of gilded wood or of porcelain designed in rococo style. In drawing rooms that date from the reign of Charles IV (1788–1808) San Ildefonso mirrors reflect light upon more formal, neoclassic interiors, as in the Pompeian-style decoration of the 'Salón de Espejos' (Salon of Mirrors) at Aranjuez. In 1764, eleven mirrors were sent by Charles III to his son, Ferdinand I, king of the Two Sicilies. Their cost was high, about 124,000 reales, because it included the value of not only the finished glasses but also replacements for plates broken during polishing and cutting. Along with the mirrors went crystal-glass vases carefully engraved with the royal arms of Sicily and Naples. Years later, Ferdinand was to

[1] Bourgoing, *op. cit.*, pp. 199–201, *tr.*
[2] J. Townsend, *A Journey through Spain in the Years 1786 and 1787*, London, 1791, vol. 2, p. 114.

receive another similar gift from his father, and in 1782 Charles presented a shipment of mirrors to the Sultan of Turkey to celebrate a treaty successfully negotiated.[1]

Apart from mirrors, chandeliers became important items in King Charles's renovations of the royal palaces. The oldest chandeliers have gilt or silvered shafts and armatures, from which hang crystal drops cut in the forms of fleurs-de-lis, ivy and oak leaves, or grape clusters. Many such early examples must have been replaced, for most of the chandeliers now in the Madrid Palace date from the reigns of Charles IV and Ferdinand VII. They have moulded and notched crystal branches hung with chains of cut-crystal drops and strings of prisms, that are like gems cut on the lapidary's wheel. A great number of these lighting fixtures are importations from England or France, but there are some from the San Ildefonso factory; among those at Madrid is a chandelier of thirty single lights (Plate 76) hanging in the antechamber of the Infanta Isabel. The shaft consists of three ormolu urns decorated with bands wrought in neoclassic designs and partially covered with crystal. The curved arms are moulded and notched, ending in flowerlike candleholders with petal-edged *bobêches*. Swags and pendant chains of faceted, pear-shaped drops sparkle between the branches. From canopies at the top and the base swing festoons of quivering drops and little sunburst plaques.

Another chandelier of about the same date (Plate 77) hangs in the royal pharmacy of the Madrid Palace. Far less elaborate, it has eight lights supported by angular and curved branches of notched crystal. The shaft is a series of moulded and cut-crystal balusters and urns rising from an octagonal metal block that is encased in crystal. The terminal pendant is a metal torch wrought with classic motifs and encircled by a ring of leaves. From the top canopy hang strings of faceted teardrops, and from each arm depends a large pear-shaped crystal. The *bobêches* are of a much later date, fan-cut in the English style of the 1820's.

When, in 1764, crystal chandeliers of twelve to sixteen lights were ordered for the Madrid Palace, the director of the Real Fábrica de Cristales replied that chandeliers of so many lights, not being saleable, had not been made at the factory for a long time. There were on hand, he wrote, four chandeliers of twelve lights, formerly considered unusable and in bad taste. Three of them and six more with eight lights he promised to equip with new branches and send to Madrid. He asked that the official palace architect send him designs so that each week four chandeliers of twelve or sixteen lights might be sent off to Madrid, in order that 'the new Royal Palace may

---

[1] Frothingham, *Hispanic Glass*, p. 106; Bourgoing, *op. cit.*, p. 201.

have suitable adornment'. Later, he reported that he was forwarding one chandelier of sixteen lights, which was 'in good taste and very large'.[1]

Lighting fixtures dating from the reign of Ferdinand VII followed the styles set by English and Irish glass factories. The fashion was that of Regency England, when chandeliers having thirty lights or more were composed of long chains of brilliantly cut drops, cascading downwards in such profusion that the shafts were completely hidden and ending in myriads of icicle prisms. In addition to chandeliers, the factory at San Ildefonso produced candelabra in floral shapes, mirrored wall sconces and single candlestick holders shaped like dolphins, flowers and palm trees. Another department of the factory was given over to grinding and polishing lenses for optical and magnifying glasses, including opera glasses and lorgnettes.

Even in Ventura Sit's lifetime the Real Fábrica de Cristales included a division for the manufacture of blown crystals, tableware and ornamental pieces decorated with cutting and engraving. News of the opportunities offered at the factory must have travelled beyond the borders of Spain, for a response came from the glass-blowers and engravers of several countries. About 1746, a Frenchman, Denis Sivert, migrated to Spain and began working at San Ildefonso. Three years later, the director of 'French crystals' was Antoine Berger who had brought with him from France a number of workmen. When he returned to his native country to recruit more glass-blowers for the Spanish factory, he was arrested for political reasons. Claude Seigne, a glassworker from Nevers, also was employed at this period by the San Ildefonso factory. From the factory of 'French crystals' Queen María Amalia, shortly before her untimely death in 1760, purchased a small carafe for thirty-five reales.[2]

From Sweden came a master glassman named Joseph Eder, who had resided in Amsterdam during 1739 and again in 1750. At San Ildefonso he received royal permission in 1754 to work in the plate glass division, making large plates that reportedly needed no polishing. Eventually, he transferred to the department producing free-blown and mould-blown crystals. There, until 1778 or longer, he supervised the workmen and experimented with formulae to produce a clear and colourless glass.[3] From this time onwards,

---

[1] Pérez Bueno, *Vidrios y vidrieras*, pp. 131, 134–5.

[2] G. Desdevises du Dezert, *Un consul général de France à Madrid sous Ferdinand VI (1748–1756)* (in *Revue hispanique*, Paris, 1907, vol. 16, p. 91); E. Gerspach, *L'Art de la verrerie*, Paris [1885], p. 304; M. T. Oliveros de Castro, *María Amalia de Sajonia, esposa de Carlos III* [Madrid] 1953, pp. 202, 434–5.

[3] Pérez Bueno, '*L'Arte vetraria*', de Neri. *Su conexión con las reales fábricas de cristales establecidos en San Ildefonso* (in *Archivo español de arte*, Madrid, 1945, vol. 18, p. 203); M. G. Suárez y Núñez, *Memorias instructivas, y curiosas*, Madrid, 1780, vol. 4, pp. 284–90 (Memorias L–LII: *Sobre el vidrio, y los esmaltes*).

the soda-lime metal of this factory gave glass that was brilliant of surface and so nearly without colour that contemporaries called it crystal. Accustomed as the modern eye is to flawless crystal, it regards the glass of San Ildefonso as having a slight tint of green or yellow, caused by impurities in the raw materials, its transparency marred by tiny bubbles, unfused particles and striations.

Eder's son Laurence, who had come to Spain with his father, worked also in the division where blown glassware was made. His job was to engrave crystals in the German manner. It would be entirely conjectural to say that Laurence had decorated the glass with the arms of the Duke of Medinaceli illustrated on Plate 81B, even though the engraving – a splendid escutcheon enclosed within crossed branches of olive and palm – has a distinctly Germanic quality. Indeed, the motif is executed in much the same style as those done earlier in the century by German craftsmen working in Sweden. Not many San Ildefonso crystals among the surviving examples of Eder's period have such elaborate wheel-engraving. More commonly they are engraved with conventional patterns in Bohemian style, as is the decanter illustrated on Plate 79. Cut in broad, rounded grooves, an even simpler design ornaments a mug (Plate 81A) shaped like the beer mugs of eighteenth-century Flanders and Holland.

Under Joseph Eder's direction, Sigismund Brun, a native of Hanover, began work as a boy at the Spanish royal factory. His first job, though menial, was the start of a long and important career. Over the years he learned all the skills of glassmaking and acquired the title of master. About 1768, he took charge of a second workshop for the manufacture of blown crystals and coloured glasses. This department he supervised for many years, since he was still its head in 1791. During his administration were manufactured a vast number of the glasses that are familiar to us now as products of the Real Fábrica de Cristales. Several engravers worked under his direction, and within the group were two or three who had French surnames.[1]

By 1798, the Fábrica de Cristales, long separated from the mirror factory, had become absorbed within the town boundaries. Three great buildings contained the furnaces, rooms for engraving and gilding and a shop where the products were sold. Crystals and coloured glasses, engraved or gilt, and shaped for many different purposes were described by the Count of Maule as being very pretty. 'As we have observed', he wrote, 'from the beauty of these objects it seems to us that they would be in great demand in America.'

[1] Gudiol Ricart and Artíñano, *op. cit.*, pp. 80–1; Larruga, *op. cit.*, 1791, vol. 13, p. 275.

For this reason, he thought than San Ildefonso glasses should be sold, not in Madrid, but in Cádiz, from which port the yearly shipments to the Indies included thousands of boxes containing German glass.[1] The suggestion to encourage the export of Spanish crystals to America echoed what many Spaniards had been advocating for almost forty years.

How to make the royal factory pay for itself became a matter of serious consideration for Charles III, and so it was that he decided to offer glasses from the royal factory for public sale. The high cost of manufacture had for a long time been a heavy drain financially on the Spanish monarchs. Materials necessary to glassmaking were expensive, due principally to the remote location of the factory. Neighbouring forests, after many years' service, became depleted of wood, and other important supplies had to be procured from distant parts of the realm at the added expense of customs duties between provinces. About 1760, a combined storeroom and shop was opened in the Puerta del Sol at Madrid. Unfortunately, this measure did not solve the problem, since customers calling there found the crystals too high-priced for their pockets. Apart from the cost of production and transportation, the breakage of glasses during the long journeys, via muleback each week from San Ildefonso to Madrid, doubled the prices on those that were left. An arbitrary reduction of twenty to thirty per cent on all crystals was ordered in 1760, and a further lowering of prices followed somewhat later in the century.[2]

An attempt to protect the products of the San Ildefonso factory came in 1762 when a royal decree granted to it the exclusive right to sell glasses in the city of Madrid and within a radius of twenty leagues around San Ildefonso. This order outlawed for the next twenty-six years the sale of crystals, except those from the King's factory, at the nation's capital (see p. 47). The directors continued to maintain a salesroom in Madrid, as well as workrooms where such terminal processes as the quicksilvering of mirrors, framing, lens-grinding and the assembling of chandeliers could be done. In 1763, two artists, José Giraldo and Blas Velilla, who had worked at the San Ildefonso establishment for many years, wished to open a shop in Madrid where they could engrave San Ildefonso glass, but the directors would not give them permission, contending that Madrid already had two shops where this glass was sold, the official salesroom and another on the Puerta del Sol. Two Spaniards, whose names are unrecorded, opened a shop in 1765 on the Calle de Toledo where they engraved mirrors and table

[1] N. de la Cruz y Bahamonde, conde de Maule, *Viage de España, Francia, e Italia,* Cádiz, 1812, vol. 12, p. 22, *tr.*
[2] Pérez Bueno, *Vidrio,* p. 520.

glasses, assembled chandeliers and constructed mirror frames, sconces and ecclesiastical furnishings from small pieces of plate glass. Later, they were joined by two of their former colleagues from San Ildefonso. As the century progressed, many glassworkers at the royal factory left and went to Madrid. There they advertised in the daily newspapers, making known their specialities in hopes of attracting a rich clientele. One of these men boldly opened a shop next door to the factory's official salesroom and put a notice in the news journal that he made and sold trick tumblers and goblets.[1] In 1785 the showrooms and shop of the Real Fábrica de Cristales were located on the old Calle del Turco, in a building which today (on the same street now renamed after the Marqués de Cubas) houses the Academia de Jurisprudencia in Madrid.[2]

Despite the combined efforts of Charles III, his minister of finance and the directors, San Ildefonso glasses did not sell. Some economics experts laid the blame on unfair competition, especially from foreign goods, but the factory directors thought that possibly a lack of sufficient sales outlets was the cause. Hopefully they agreed to a proposal from the nation's board of commerce that a shipment of San Ildefonso crystals be sent to New Spain, a scheme approved by King Charles in 1760. The factory treasurer hurried to Cádiz with crystals worth one million reales, which he was to consign to a vessel of the Indies Fleet, bound for Vera Cruz. Before he reached Cádiz, the Fleet had sailed. Hastily changing plans, he put the glasses on board a merchant vessel sailing for Havana – a shipment containing mirrors with engraved frames, crystal sconces fitted with brackets and branches to hold candles, drinking glasses of every kind, decanters and cruets.[3]

From start to finish the venture fared badly. The port and packing charges had been high, and upon the return of the Fleet in December of the following year, the directors learned that the proceeds from sales were computed as 199,500 reales, although the original worth of the glasses had been reckoned as over five times that amount. In New Spain, the colonials had not fancied the glasses chosen at the factory, partly because the objects were not boxed in assortments.[4]

An idea of the kind of glasses that would have been included in such an assortment comes from a set of San Ildefonso crystals now belonging to the Missouri Historical Society of Saint Louis. Originally the pieces numbered

[1] Pérez Bueno, *Vidrio*, pp. 530–2.
[2] F. de Llanos y Torriglia, '*Año de 1801*'; *la casa de Heros*, Madrid [1920], pp. 15–16.
[3] Pérez Bueno, *Vidrio*, pp. 527–8.
[4] J. Guillot Carratalá, *Los vidrios*, Madrid, 1957, pp. 15–16 (Temas españolas, no. 293); Larruga, *op. cit.* 1791, vol. 13, pp. 275–8.

forty packed together in a chest, but, after a fire that destroyed most of them in 1914, only nine remain (Plate 91). They are flat-bottomed tumblers of two sizes, probably for water and dinner wines, glasses for sherry or port, salt dishes, a pepper shaker, a castor perhaps for sugar, and two other receptacles for condiments. Each glass is decorated with a matching flower, engraved and gilt. Traditionally the set is believed to have been the property of Pierre Laclède, a French merchant-trader of New Orleans and founder of Saint Louis. In 1770, a few years after the establishment of the city, Spain sent Pedro Piernas there to act as lieutenant-governor of its territory in Upper Louisiana. Thus, it may be that the glasses associated with Saint Louis belonged to Piernas or one of his fellow officers. The rococo style of the floral pattern on these San Ildefonso glasses coincides nicely with this period of history.

During the latter part of the eighteenth century, the crystals of San Ildefonso were often packed into travelling cases, like the set now in the Museo Arqueológico Nacional at Madrid. The wooden case is decorated outside with a stylized pattern; on the inside, it is lined with contemporary green damask woven in a floral design. Closely fitted into the box are decanters of two sizes, for wines and spirits, together with goblets and tumblers. The crystal glasses are ornamented in fire-gilt with grapevine motifs that indicate a date near 1785.

The discovery of a method for firing gilt on glass has been accredited to Sigismund Brun. From the great quantity of gilt-decorated glasses turned out by his department of the factory, we become convinced that he either invented the process used at San Ildefonso or improved upon a standard formula. The general principle in fire-gilding at that period was to paint on the outer surface of glass with a brush dipped into a mixture of gold-leaf ground up with honey. The metal was fixed to the glass by firing in a muffle and was then brightened by burnishing. Such work done by Brun and his men has survived remarkably well, the gilt patterns still shining with their original lustre. Often on his glasses the gilding was used to accentuate engraved patterns, covering all motifs engraved by the wheel. There also occurred gilt designs painted directly on the uncut surface of the glass. Charges from the royal arms of Spain are painted in this way and combined with rings of cut beading round a covered bowl (Plate 89A). The gilt castles, lions, pomegranates and the fleurs-de-lis of the Bourbon dynasty are painted carefully in silhouette, with fine details incised with a point through the gold.

The progress of eighteenth-century design from rococo to neoclassic may be followed in the engraved-and-gilt patterns that decorate glasses from the San Ildefonso factory. Twice repeated across a covered jar (Plate 78) sweeps a rococo pattern of floral sprays, drawn with charming freedom of line and an abundance of attractive detail. The large size of the jar with its exaggeratedly high cover surprises the observer, another trick of rococo designers. Readily seen on the jar is the method by which the gold deposit is spread thinly across broad surfaces of engraving and filled thickly into the deeper cuts. Blossoms resembling the heads of sunflowers decorate a tapered decanter (Plate 82) of English shape and a sugar bowl (Plate 88) with domed cover and low foot. Smaller flowers, drawn on gracefully curved stems and arranged loosely in naturalistic sprays, ornament a tumbler, a bottle and a bell-shaped wineglass (Plates 86A–B). These glasses, flower-sprinkled in the rococo manner, are but a few of the many that may be cited as having come from the San Ildefonso factory.

As the last decade of the century approached, a neoclassic decoration emerged, supplanting the freely drawn patterns of earlier years. Designs became less imaginative, being limited to a few formal motifs in stiff combinations. These traits are evident in the interwoven band round a salt dish (Plate 86B), in the floral garlands encircling a wineglass (Plate 85B). Somewhat less schematic are the floral-and-ribbon swags, the stars and the chains on a sugar bowl (Plate 89B); although stylized, the basket of flowers engraved on a small tray (Plate 87) has some semblance of reality.

A publication of 1780 proves that the glassmen at San Ildefonso experimented with many formulae for coloured metals, opaque-white glass and enamels.[1] By royal order, Miguel Jerónimo Suárez began in 1774 a Spanish translation of Antonio Neri's treatise on glass, taken from the French edition of 1752, incorporating the notes of Merret and Kunckel. Several manuscript copies were made for the use of workers at San Ildefonso who could read only their native language.[2] To present recent material on glass-making, the translator included comments on Neri's methods, given by some of the most able and experienced masters in the factory. José Piquer, an assistant to Eder, and José Busquet recorded also what materials and methods they themselves favoured for making coloured glasses. Since they showed great familiarity with formulae used by Catalan glass-blowers, it seems probable that both men came to San Ildefonso from Cataluña.

In judging Neri's mixture of antimony, nitre and common glass for making a white enamel, Busquet recognized the Italian formula as the basis for coloured enamels in Cataluña and remarked that he had success-fully made use of Kunckels' annotation to this formula. An alternative

[1] Suárez, *op. cit.*, pp. 185–468.  [2] Pérez Bueno, '*L'Arte vetraria*', pp. 204–8.

method, preferred by the masters of San Ildefonso, produced 'a glass that looks like porcelain, by means of which are made, with great beauty, all the opaque colours.' The chief ingredients were white sand, refined potash and bone ash. Although the mixture looked clear as it came from the crucible, it turned opalescent or milky on cooling. Another formula for opaque-white glass was composed of crystal pot-metal, to which were added tin oxide, lead oxide and manganese. 'This milk colour is produced very perfectly at San Ildefonso and with it are made various pieces imitating the porcelain of Saxony.'[1]

The royal factory made drinking glasses of milk white and other opaque colours shaped like small barrels with the tops and the bases encircled by blue, red or white threadings to represent hoops. Several examples formerly in the Riaño collection now belong to the Victoria and Albert Museum, and there are many more scattered about in museums and private collections everywhere. The formulae for tinting glass blue or green were numerous in the Suárez translation of Neri. Thus, it is not surprising to find cobalt, emerald and aquamarine among the coloured glasses that may be attributed to the San Ildefonso factory. Of this kind are three pocket tumblers, blown and flattened to oval shape (Plate 80); the first, of cobalt blue, has combed white stripes, made by trailing white cords horizontally around the soft gather on a blowpipe, marvering these cords flat and dragging across them a sharp-pointed tool. The amethyst glass in the centre is painted with a delicate fire-gilt pattern and inscribed with the name of Vitoriana Baquero. A similar tumbler, blown of cobalt-blue glass, once belonged to another member of the Baquero family, Da Claudia; it is now in the collection of the Victoria and Albert Museum. The third glass illustrated on Plate 80 simulates a blue stone spotted with white. Workers at the royal factory excelled in making these speckled glasses to imitate chalcedony, agate, jasper and other semiprecious stones.

Crystal, blue and milk-white glasses decorated with enamels were produced in quantities at San Ildefonso. They are closely related to the engraved glasses in ornamentation, shape and quality.[2] Painted in pastel colours, the designs are garden flowers of rose-pink, apricot, cerulean and sapphire blues, yellow and white; pale green serves for the foliage. Working as though in oils, the painters blended their colours to give variations in hue and tonality, tracing details or outlining forms with dark shades or with black. Arranged in wreaths, bouquets and garlands, the flowers are

---

[1] Suárez, op. cit., pp. 289–90, 317, tr., 354–5, tr.
[2] Frothingham, Enameled Glass from the Spanish Royal Factory (in Journal of Glass Studies, vol. III, Corning [N. Y.], 1961, pp. 118–29).

recognizable as roses, tulips and daisies, pansies and violets, forget-me-nots and lilies-of-the-valley.

The design on a covered jar (Colour plate D), clearly and precisely drawn, shows how attractive enamelled decoration could be when a talented painter held the brush. Typically Spanish, San Ildefonso jars of this shape seem to have been exceedingly popular. They vary slightly from one piece to another (Plate 96), being spherical or ovoid, topped by a prominent, cylindrical collar and set on a low foot of solid glass. The handles, either rods or straps, curve downwards from the collar with the ends pinched off and pressed against the bulge below. A cone-shaped cover, with its edge folded to form a guard, is topped by a knob or a mushroom. The covered jar was a favourite shape also for decorating with engraved and gilt designs.

Usually enamel-painting at the royal factory was done in a soft careless manner, as most of the illustrated glasses show. The shapes, like those of their engraved counterparts, ran to decanters (Plate 83) and wineglasses (Plate 85A) of English shape, large mugs for beer or cider (Plate 90A) and smaller glasses for wine (Plate 85A-B). The mugs, of crystal, blue, green or milk-white glass, were either straight-sided or waisted (Plates 84A–B) with flaring brims. Brandy glasses also were painted with bright flowers, one in the Hermitage Museum, Leningrad, being decorated with a floral wreath based on an engraved and gilt design (Plate 90B).

The archives of the Ministerio de Hacienda and of the Royal Palace, Madrid, contain documents that name a few artists who painted simultaneously for the Buen Retiro porcelain factory and the San Ildefonso glassworks. This exchange of talent seems epitomized in a series of neoclassic urns, intended as drug jars for the Madrid Palace pharmacy, some of porcelain and others of crystal glass (Plate 92). The order for them was signed by Godoy as Secretary of State in 1794.[1] The proportions of the moulded jars indicate that they follow the same model, a classic shape familiar to the silversmith. There is a similarity, also, in the enamelled and gilt decorations on both porcelain and glass – the escutcheon of Charles IV surmounted by an imperial crown and encircled by crossed branches of palm and olive. On the ovolo mouldings which run round the edge of the cover are painted green laurel leaves bound by blue and white ribbons. Gilding brightens the knobs on the covers, the mouldings and alternate gadroons. Among the enamel-painters of porcelain and glass was a man named Antonio Martínez, who appeared on the Buen Retiro rosters from

[1] Their cost was 287, 428 reales vellon. M. Pérez Villamil, *Artes é industrias del Buen Retiro*, Madrid, 1904, pp. 44, 83, 86, 143, 145, 148; Llanos y Torriglia, *op. cit.*, pp. 18–19.

D. *Covered jar, with enamelled and fire-gilt decorations.*
*La Granja de San Ildefonso, about* 1775-85. *Ht.* 12 *in.* (30.6 *cm.*)
*The Corning Museum of Glass, Corning (New York)*
(*See page* 84)

1785 to 1804. Since he was so employed during the year when the urns were ordered for the Palace pharmacy, he may have been their decorator.

At this period, an engraver in the San Ildefonso factory, Félix Ramos, recorded himself for posterity by signing a rectangular plaque (Plate 94) with his name and the statement that he had engraved it. Probably copying the subject from a print, Ramos executed his wheel-engraving with infinite care and precision on the crystal pane. The inscription identifies the view as the façade of the Palace of La Granja, seen from the gardens. Each tiny detail of architecture is cut clearly and delicately into the surface. The interwoven strands of flowers and foliage framing the picture indicate a date within the last decade of the century.

The style of glass-cutting and engraving changed radically about 1800. Suddenly the fashion was for heavy glasses mitre-cut and fan-cut in the Anglo-Irish manner. The Spanish pieces as they came from the engraver's wheel could not compare with their models for sparkle and prismatic colour, primarily because the quality of Spanish crystal did not equal that of English 'flint' glass. In addition to the mitre-cutting, one finds a decoration of hastily sketched floral motifs drawn in gilt. Of these glasses there exist small bowls, hemispherical or bell-shaped, standing on heavy plinths cut with vertical facets (Plates 93A–B). A San Ildefonso goblet of Regency shape belongs to the Macaya collection at Barcelona. Decorated in gilt, probably for Charles IV or a member of the royal family, the goblet, which stands on a star-cut plinth, displays the Spanish coat of arms enwreathed in grapevines.

Set up as King of Spain in 1808 by the victorious Napoleon, Joseph Bonaparte began a reign that was to last for the next five years. On the 23rd of September, 1809, he made public a decree concerning the glass factory of San Ildefonso. The system of royal patronage followed by his predecessors to subsidize industries, he considered futile, causing industry to stagnate. 'Desirous of opening new ways toward national prosperity', Joseph offered the Real Fábrica de Cristales and its storerooms in Madrid for sale to private industry. The Minister of the Interior was to take charge of the arrangements; companies or individuals could buy the furnishings, machines and tools of the factory, either to carry on manufacture at the original location or to transport them elsewhere. If the glass factory should remain at San Ildefonso, the owners might purchase wood from the hills near the royal estate, for which privilege they would pay a fee to the crown. Glassmen interested in renting the houses, buildings and storerooms from the crown might do so. Former glassworkers already pensioned and those employed when this decree was issued, of whom there were nearly three hundred, would enjoy pensions for life. The commission liquidating the credits would see that all creditors were paid, and salaries owed to the workmen were to be paid from the sale of the factory furnishings.[1]

Two months later the Minister ordered that all glasses of every kind be classified and appraised, amounting to 327,195 pieces. By the time that State officials and Joseph Bonaparte had received their portions of the proceeds and the salaries had been paid, there was left to be divided among the creditors only the unsold glassware.[2]

By July of 1809, the Madrid shop on the Calle del Turco had already closed its doors to the public; but within two years, an advertisement appeared in the *Diario* to the effect that the Real Fábricas de Cristales had established a shop in the Portal de Paños for wholesale and retail trade, to be managed by two masters from the factory, Juan Sarriet and Antonio Juan. This announcement indicates that glasses were still being produced at San Ildefonso, although under private management. The factory did not restrict the sale of its goods to this one outlet, since in May of the same year another shop, located on the 'Street of the Germans', opened its doors to sell plate glass, bottles, tumblers, goblets and all shapes of glassware of fine or ordinary quality.[3]

Upon the withdrawal of Napoleon's army from Spain, the rightful King Ferdinand VII returned to Madrid in 1814. He had not long resumed his throne before he attempted to reinstate the former royal factories, that of San Ildefonso being among them. For several years work progressed, although on a restricted scale, and the old shop in Madrid re-opened on the Calle de Toledo to sell San Ildefonso crystals to the public.[4] Examples of crystal tumblers and other drinking glasses of this period, now in the Museo Arqueológico Nacional, Madrid, are moulded or mould-blown and engraved with romantic landscapes, floral wreaths, military trophies and the names of their former owners – Teresa Texedor, María Gutiérrez and the like. Once in a while they bear a date, as does a tumbler inscribed, 'Mem[ori]a de M[adrid] 1816'.

More important work was done for the royal palaces, principally mirrors, chandeliers and decorative glasses. A most unusual piece is a tea-table or lamp-stand, of which the crystal-glass top shows diamond- and prism-cutting (Plate 95). A circular medallion in the centre, left smooth and uncut,

[1] *Gazeta de Madrid*, 1 October, 1809. pp. 1209–10; J. B. J. Breton de la Martinière, *L'Espagne et le Portugal*, Paris, 1815, vol. 5, p. 223.
[2] Llanos y Torriglia, *op. cit.* pp. 20–1.
[3] *Diario de Madrid*, 14 July, 1809, p. 55; 21 February, 1811, p. 212; 24 May, 1811, p. 580.
[4] Marqués de Lozoya, *Historia del arte hispánico*, Barcelona, etc., 1949, vol. 5, p. 147; *Paseo por Madrid, ó Guía del forastero en la corte*, Madrid, 1815, p. 93.

is painted with an allegorical theme portraying Peace and the Muse of the choral dance, Terpsichore with her lyre. Between these figures two cherubs hold up an oval plaque surmounted by the royal crown; on it are inscribed the interlaced initials, M J A, for Queen María Josefa Amalia, third wife of Ferdinand VII. The little table may thus be dated between 1819, the year of her marriage, and 1829, the year of her death. The medallion has been attributed to a Court Painter, Vicente López, the same artist who in 1825 painted an allegorical fresco on the ceiling of the Salón de Carlos III in the Madrid Palace. The mounting for the table is ormolu wrought at the Royal Factory of Silversmiths in Madrid.[1] Probably this odd piece of furniture was among the last of the important pieces produced under royal patronage, since in 1829 the San Ildefonso factory was rented to a private company. After the reign of Isabel II, various commercial enterprises have taken over the factory but without financial success. On several occasions manufacture has been abandoned for long periods of time, only to be revived for a brief renascence, like that in 1845 when San Ildefonso products made a brilliant showing at the Exposición Industrial.[2]

[1] Information supplied by the Patrimonio Nacional, Madrid.
[2] Lozoya, *op. cit.* p. 148; J. de Fagoaga and T. Muñico, *Descripción de los reales sitios de San Ildefonso, Valsain y Riofrio*, Segovia, 1845, p. 195–6.

BURGOS
★

VALLADOLID
★

QUEJIGAL
★

SEGOVIA
★
SAN ILDEFONSO★
AVILA★
CEBREROS★              EL
                    ★ ESCORIAL        GU
GUISANDO        ★VALDEMAQUEL
          SAN MARTIN        ★MADRID
              ★ DE
CADALSO     ★VALDEIGLESIAS
DE LOS      TORRE DE
VIDRIOS     ESTEBAN
            HAMBRAN

                              PINAR DE LA V
CORDOBA
★                           JAEN       CA
CALA★                        ★
                    VALDEPEÑAS
          ★          CABRA ★
SEVILLA
                              GRANADA
                                ★

CADIZ ★

GLASS  CEN

# BIBLIOGRAPHY

GENERAL

J. F. Riaño y Montero, *Classified and Descriptive Catalogue of the Art Objects of Spanish Production* (Victoria and Albert Museum), London, 1872.

M. Rico y Sinobas, *Del vidrio y sus artífices en España*, Madrid, 1873.

A. Nesbitt, *A Descriptive Catalogue of the Glass Vessels in the South Kensington Museum*, London, 1878.

J. F. Riaño y Montero, *The Industrial Arts in Spain*, London, 1st edition, 1879, pp. [228]–249.

L. Williams, *The Arts and Crafts of Older Spain* (The World of Art Series), Chicago, Edinburgh, 1908, vol. 2, pp. 223–[263].

E. A. Barber, *Spanish Glass in the Collection of The Hispanic Society of America*, New York and London, 1917.

J. Gudiol y Cunill, *Catàlech dels vidres que integren la colecció Amatller*, Barcelona, 1925.

J. Gudiol Ricart, *Vidres de la col·lecció Amatller* (extract from Associació Catalana d'Antropología, Etnología i Prehistòria, *Butlletí*, vol. 4, Barcelona, 1926, pp. 122–9).

B. Rackham, *Glass* (in *Spanish Art*, Burlington Magazine Monograph, no. 2, New York, 1927, pp. 85–6).

L. Pérez Bueno, *Vidrio* (in *Folklore y costumbres de España*, edited by F. Carreras y Candi, vol. 2, Barcelona, 1931, pp. [419]–534).

J. Gudiol Ricart and P. M. de Artíñano y Galdácano, *Vidrio: Resumen de la historia del vidrio; Catálogo de la colección Alfonso Macaya*, Barcelona, 1935.

L. Pérez Bueno, *Vidrios españoles en el extranjero, siglos XVI, XVII y XVIII* (in Cuerpo Facultativo de Archiveros, Bibliotecarios y Arqueólogos, *Anuario*, vol. 3, Madrid, 1935, pp. [195]–205).

A. W. Frothingham, *Hispanic Glass, with Examples in the Collection of The Hispanic Society of America*, New York, 1941.

L. Pérez Bueno, *Vidrios y vidrieras* (Artes decorativas españolas), Barcelona, 1942.

# Bibliography

L. Pérez Bueno, *Los vidrios en España* (Publicaciones de la Escuela de Artes y Oficios Artísticos de Madrid, no. 14), [Madrid] 1943.

W. B. Honey, *Glass; a Handbook . . . & a Guide to the Museum Collection* (Victoria and Albert Museum), London, 1946, pp. 144–7.

[M. L. Herrera Escudero] *Colección de vidrios españoles* (in Cuerpo Facultativo de Archiveros, Bibliotecarios y Arqueólogos, *Adquisiciones del Museo Arqueológico Nacional (1940–1945)*. Madrid, 1947, pp. 197–201).

L. Planell, *Vidrio; historia, tradición y arte*, 2 vols., Barcelona, 1948.

M. Oliva Prat, *Catálogo de los vidrios del Museo Arqueológico de Gerona*, [Gerona] 1950.

J. Ainaud de Lasarte, *Cerámica y vidrio* (Ars Hispaniae vol. 10), Madrid [1952] pp. 345–73.

J. Guillot Carratalá, *Los vidrios* (Temas españoles, no. 293), Madrid, 1957.

G. Mariacher, *La raccolta dei vetri spagnoli al Museo Vetrario di Murano*, Venice, 1958 (offprint from *Giornale economico*, June 1958).

M. C. Quaresma, *Contribuição para o estudo dos vidros do Museu Nacional de Soares dos Reis* (in *Museu*, ser. 2, no. 1, Porto, 1960, pp. 63–7).

[M. Braña] *Colección de vidrios de la Edad Moderna* (in Cuerpo Facultativo de Archiveros, Bibliotecarios y Arqueólogos, *Memorias de los museos arqueológicos, 1955 a 57 (extractos)*, vols. XVI–XVIII, Madrid, 1960, pp. 92–5).

### CHAPTERS 1–2

Saint Quirin, *Les verriers du Languedoc, 1290–1790* (in Société Languedocienne de Géographie, *Bulletin*, Montpellier, 1904–6, vol. 27, pp. [177]–198, [285]–326; vol. 28, pp. [35]–86, [166]–204, [265]–290, [339]–384; vol. 29, pp. [35]–83, [149]–203).

J. Folch y Torres, *Els antics vidres catalans esmaltats* (El tresor artistic de Catalunya, sèrie B, secció 4), Barcelona [1926].

S. Capdevila, *La industria vidriera a Tarragona* (in Societat Arqueológica Tarraconense, *Butlletí arqueològic*, època 3, Tarragona, 1933, pp. 243–4).

E. Toda y Güell, *La col·lecció de vidres antics de Poblet* (in Societat Arqueológica Tarraconense, *Butlletí arqueològic*, època 3, Tarragona, 1935, pp. 46–9).

J. Gudiol Ricart, *Els vidres catalans* (Monumenta Cataloniæ, vol. 3), Barcelona [1936].

J. Amades, *El porró* (Arte popular), Barcelona, 1938.

J. Gudiol y Cunill, *De vidrios esmaltados catalanes*, tr. from *De vidres*

# Bibliography

*esmaltats catalans* in *La Veu de Catalunya* (in L. Planell, *Vidrio; historia, tradición y arte*, vol. 2, Barcelona, 1948, pp. 77–[93]).

M. Sanchis Guarner, *El arte del vidrio en Mallorca* (Panorama balear, no. 16), [Palma, 1952].

F. Almela y Vives, *La antigua industria del vidrio en Valencia*, Valencia, 1954.

A. W. Frothingham, *Barcelona Glass in Venetian Style*, New York 1956.

## CHAPTER 3

J. Eguaras Ibáñez, *Museo Arqueológico de Granada; Colección de vidrios andaluces* (in Cuerpo Facultativo de Archiveros, Bibliotecarios y Arqueólogos, *Memorias de los museos arqueológicos provinciales, 1948–9* (*extractos*). vols. IX–X. Madrid, 1950, pp. 289–96).

## CHAPTER 4

E. Larruga y Boneta, *Memorias políticas y económicas sobre los frutos, comercio, fábricas y minas de España*, Madrid, 1791–2, vol. 10, pp. 53–63, vol. 16, pp. 222–3, vol. 19, pp. 260–93.

P. M. de Artíñano y Galdácano, *La fabricación de vidrios en el Nuevo Baztán* (in *Arte español*, vol. 10, Madrid, 1929, pp. 427–9).

## CHAPTER 5

A. Ponz, *Viaje de España*, 1st edition, 1781, Madrid, 1947, vol. 10, letter 7, pp. 905–6.

Larruga y Boneta, *op. cit.*, Madrid, 1791, vol. 13, pp. 274–9.

J. de Fagoaga and T. Muñico, *Descripción de los reales sitios de San Ildefonso, Valsain y Riofrio*, Segovia, 1845, pp. 192–200.

M. Rico y Sinobas, *Espejos y vasos labrados de fábricas españolas que se conservan en la colección del Ilmo. Sr. D. Manuel Rico y Sinobas* (in *Museo español de antigüedades*, vol. 9, Madrid, 1878, pp. [515]–520).

C. de Lecea y García, *Recuerdos de la antigua industria segoviana*, Segovia, 1897, pp. [199]–212.

L. Pérez Bueno, *Real Fábrica de cristales de San Ildefonso (La Granja); antecedentes y apuntes para su historia* (in *Arte español*, vol. 8. Madrid, 1926, pp. 9–15).

L. Pérez Bueno, '*L'Arte vetraria*', de Neri. *Su conexión con las reales fábricas de cristales establecidas en San Ildefonso* (in *Archivo español de arte*, vol. 18, Madrid, 1945, pp. 201–18, 312).

A. W. Frothingham, *Enameled Glass from the Spanish Royal Factory* (in *Journal of Glass Studies*, vol. III, Corning [N. Y.], 1961, pp. 118–29).

# INDEX

Abolais, 13–14
Albión, Violante, 31, 32
Alburquerque, duke of, 33, 41, 60–1
Alcalá de Henares (Madrid), 66
Alcalá la Real (Jaén), 53
Alcañiz (Teruel), 74
Alcira (Valencia), 47
Alfonso V, king of Aragón, 24
Alfonso X, king of Castilla, 13–14
Alhama (Murcia), 26
Alicante, 11–12, 36, 47, 59, 64
*almagro*, 75
Almatret (Lérida), 51
Almería, 13, 52, 55, 57
*almorratxa*, 22, 32, 41, 48–9
Altamira, countess of, 33, 60
Altare (Italy), 34
Amat, Bartomeu, abbot, 39
Amatller collection, Barcelona, 9, 39, 40
Anne of Austria, queen consort of Philip II, 35
Antwerp, 14, 16
Aranjuez palace, 75
Arbeteta (Guadalajara), 68
Arenales factory *see* Castril
Armallones (Guadalajara), 68
Arroyo de los Molinos (Jaén), 53
*L'Arte vetraria see* Neri
Artíñano collection, Madrid, 9
Artois, countess of, 21

Baar, Armand, collection, 10
Bailén (Jaén), 53
Bañolas, Monastery of San Esteban, 19
Barcelona, 15, 26–7, 30 ff, 54, 57, 58, 61, 64, 68
    Council, 24, 35, 45–6
    glass fairs, 23, 35
    glass furnaces, 20, 24, 32–3, 46
    Instituto Amatller de Arte Hispánico, 9, 39, 40
    Museos de Arte, 9, 36, 39
barilla, 11–12, 15, 26, 27, 36, 47, 64, 73
Barovier, Domingo, 34, 62
Barovier family, 34
Berger, Antoine, 77
Bernui (Segovia), sand from, 73
Beteta (Cuenca), 68
Biringuccio, 14–15
La Bisbal (Gerona), 51
Boix collection, Madrid, 9

Bonaparte, Joseph, king of Spain, 85, 86
Boston, Museum of Fine Arts, 19
Botia factory *see* María (Almería)
*botijo*, 56
Brescia (Italy), 34
British Museum, 10, 36–7, 55
Brun, Sigismund, 78, 81
Brussels, 63
Buen Retiro porcelain factory, 84–5
Burgo, Tomás del, 66
Burgos, 26
    Cathedral, 68
Busot (Alicante), 47

Cabot collection, Barcelona, 9
Cabra (Córdoba), 58
Cadalso de los Vidrios (Toledo), 26, 33, 57, 60–5
    Sáez factory, 71
    Villena factories, 61, 71
Cádiz, 58, 59, 79, 80
Cala (Huelva), 58
*caldereta*, 38–9
*càntir*, 48–9, 50, 51
Carolina (Jaén), 53
Cartagena (Murcia), 52, 64
Caspe (Zaragoza), 25, 48
Castilla, arms, 31
Castril de la Peña (Granada), 52, 54, 55, 56
    Arenales factory, 53
Cebreros (Avila), 62
Central European glass, 58–9
chandeliers, 50, 76–7, 79–80, 86
Charles V, emperor of the Holy Roman Empire, king of Spain, 14, 31, 33, 58
Charles III, king of Spain, 47, 70, 73, 75–6, 79, 80
    arms, 59
Charles IV, king of Spain, 75, 76, 85
    arms, 59, 84
Charleston, R. J., 22
Cieza (Murcia), 64
cold-gilding, 28
Corbera de Llobregat (Barcelona), 45
Córdoba, 13, 57
Cosimo I de'Medici, 11–12
Cristales, Real Fábrica de *see* San Ildefonso (Segovia)
Crivillén (Aragón), 48
cross, Maltese, 39
crown glass, 16

Cruilles (Gerona), 24, 51
crystals, 47, 48, 51, 62, 65 ff, 72 ff
  English-style, 49, 67, 76, 77, 84, 85
  Flemish, 14
  French, 66, 77
  German-style, 51, 70, 78
  Venetian, 34–7, 40, 42, 54, 61, *see also*
    Venetian glasses; Venetian-style glas-
    ses
Cuenca glass, 68
cut decoration, 75, 76, 77, 81–2, 85, 86–7

'Damascus' glass, 17, 22–3, 27, 41
Danis, Juan, 63
*De la pirotechnica*, treatise, 15
Desamparados, Virgin of, 47
diamond-point engraving, 40, 42
Dorado, Diego, 69
Dorado glass factory *see* Recuenco
Dowling, John, 74

Eder, Joseph, 77–8
Eder, Laurence, 78
Elche (Alicante), 25–6
enamelled decoration, 22–3, 27, 28–9, 31–2,
  36–9, 41, 59, 82–4
engraved decoration *see* diamond-point engraving; wheel engraving
Engravers of glass, 77, 78, 79, 85
El Escorial (Madrid), 34, 62, 63, 64
*estilo Isabel*, 31

Ferdinand III, king of Castilla, 57
Ferdinand V, king of Spain, 14, 27, 30, 60
Ferdinand VII, king of Spain, 73, 76, 77,
  86, 87
Ferdinand I, king of the Two Sicilies, 75
Fernández de Córdoba, Diego, 33, 68
Fernando of Austria, cardinal-infante, 45
Figueras (Gerona), 33, 51
fire-gilding, 78, 81
Flemish glass, 14, 65
Flix (Tarragona), 25
Florence (Italy), 11–12, 33
Fortuny, Mariano, 54
French-Catalan glass, 49
Fronvila, Pedro, 72
frosted glass *see* ice-glass

Las Gabarras (Gerona), 51
Garcilaso de la Vega, 60
Garzoni, Tommaso, 15
Gerona, 51
  Museo Diocesano, 19
Gil, Pere, 15, 17, 30, 36
gilding *see* cold-gilding; fire gilding
Glasgow, Kelvingrove Art Gallery, 10
'glass disease', 69
glassmakers, Andalusian, 53, 57–8
  Aragonese, 48
  Castillian, 26, 61, 63–4, 66–8, 72, 86

Catalan, 20–1, 24–5, 44, 46, 47, 51, 63,
  72, 82–3
  Dutch, 59
  English, 12, 67
  Flemish, 62–3
  French, 66–7, 77
  German, 70, 78
  Italian *see* glassmakers, Venetian
  Italo-Flemish, 62–3
  Jewish, 26
  Mallorcan, 20–1, 48
  Moorish, 26
  Roussillonais, 21, 24–5, 44
  Sevillian, 57–8
  Swedish, 77–8
  Valencian, 25–6, 46, 47
  Venetian, 34, 62–3
Godoy, Secretary of State, 84
Gondomar, Count, ambassador to England,
  62
Gothic decoration, 31–2
Goyeneche, Juan de, 66–8
Granada, 54, 55, 57
  Cathedral, 31
La Granja de San Ildefonso *see* San Ildefonso
Granollers del Vallés (Barcelona), 24
Guardia de Montserrat (Barcelona), 45
Gudiol y Cunill, José, 21
guilds of glassmakers, 14, 20, 23–4, 35,
  45–6
Guisando (Avila), 26

Hambrán *see* Torre de Esteban Hambrán
Havana, 80
Hermitage Museum *see* Leningrad
Herranz, Francisco, 64
Hinojares (Jaén), 53
The Hispanic Society of America *see* New
  York
Hispano-Muslim glass, 13–14
Hispano-Roman glass, 11–12
*Historia natural de Catalunya*, 15
Holy Sepulchre, Order of the, arms, 37, 39
Horta (Tarragona), clay from, 73
Howell, James, 12

ice-glass, 39–40, 42, 56
I H S, monogram, 39
inscriptions, 32, 39, 55, 85, 86
Isabel I, queen of Spain, 14, 27, 30–1, 32,
  39, 60
Isabel II, queen of Spain, 87
Isabel Farnese, queen-consort of Philip V
  of Spain, 67, 72
Isidore, Saint, bp. of Sevilla, 12
Islamic-type decoration, 27, 37, 55

Jaulín (Zaragoza), 48
John V, king of Portugal, arms, 59
Juana, daughter of Isabel I, 32
La Junquera (Gerona), 51

# Index

Kelvingrove Art Gallery *see* Glasgow
Kunckel's annotations to Neri, 82–3

Laclède, Pierre, 81
Lambotte, Dieudonné, 63
Lambotte, Thierry, 63
lamp, glass made at the, 17, 48, 50
Lanna, Adalbert von, collection, Prague, 37
*El lapidario*, treatise, 13–14
Lastras de Cuéllar (Segovia), sand from, 73
*latticinio* glass, 15, 40–1, 43, 45, 49, 50, 51, 58, 65–6
Leningrad, Hermitage Museum, 10, 41, 84
Liège, Musée Curtius, 10
Lisbon, 62
London *see* British Museum; Victoria and Albert Museum
López de Aragón, Fernando, 69
López, Vicente, court painter, 87

Macaya collection, Barcelona, 28, 39, 68, 85
Madrid, 55, 62, 63, 66, 67
  Academia de Jurisprudencia, 80
  Exposición Industrial, 1845, 87
  glass furnace, 62
  Museo Arqueológico Nacional, 9, 72, 81, 86
  Museo de Artes Decorativas, 9
  Patrimonio Nacional, 9, 87
  Real Academia de Bellas Artes de San Fernando, 67
  Royal Factory of Silversmiths, 87
  Royal Palace, 9, 62, 67, 70, 75, 76, 84, 87
    Pharmacy, 69, 70, 76, 84–5
  Salesrooms, 51, 63, 67, 69, 79–80, 86
Málaga, 13
Mallorca *see* Palma de Mallorca
Manresa (Barcelona), 50
  Fabrica de Vidrios Cristalinos de Bacarisas, 51
  Ubach's factory, 51
Mansell, Sir Robert, 12
María (Almería), 53–4, 55
María of Hungary, governor of the Netherlands, 14
María Amalia, queen-consort of Charles III of Spain, 77
María Josefa Amalia, queen-consort of Ferdinand VII, of Spain, 87
Marimón, Felipe, bp. of Ampurias, 39
Marineo, Lucio, 26–7, 60
Martin I, king of Aragón, 22
Martínez, Antonio, 84
Mataró (Barcelona), 24, 45, 50–1
Mateu collection, Peralada, 9
Medici, Cosimo I de', 11–12
Medina del Campo, fairs, 62
Medinaceli, arms, 78
Mendoza, Antonio de, 1st viceroy to New Spain, 58
Merret's annotations to Neri, 82

'metals' (molten glass), 11, 15, 45, 54, 56, 67, 78, 82–3
*millefiori*, 61
Miotti, Antonio, 63
mirrors, 17, 23, 62, 63, 66, 72, 73–6, 79–80, 86
Moncada (Barcelona), 24
Montserrat, Monastery of, arms, 39
mould-blown and moulded glass, 13, 20, 28, 41–3, 50, 77, 84, 86
Mudejar decoration, 28, 32
muff glass, 16, 17, 72
Mur, Church of Santa María, 19
Murano, 11–12, 15, 33, 34, 36, 40, 58, 62; *see also* Venetian glasses
  Museo Vetrario, 39
Murcia, 13, 26, 64
Murviedro (Valencia), 25

Namur, 63
Navagero, Andrea, ambassador from Venice, 31
Neri, Antonio, 16, 64, 82–3
Nevers, 77
New York, The Hispanic Society of America, 9, 10, 37–8
Nuevo Baztán glass factory, 66–8, 72

Ollería (Valencia), 47

painted decoration *see* enamelled decoration
Palau-del-Vidre (Roussillon), 21, 24, 44
Palma de Mallorca, 20–1, 27, 34, 39, 48, 62
El Pardo Palace (Madrid), 34, 36, 40, 61
Paterna (Valencia), 28
Pellizari, Antonio, 62
Peñalba (Huesca), 48
Peralada *see* Mateu collection
Peréz Bueno collection, Madrid, 9
Perpignan, 21, 25
Peter IV, king of Aragón, 23
pharmacy glasses, 22, 25, 47, 48, 50, 51, 69, 70, 84–5
Philip II, king of Spain, 14, 34–5, 39–40, 41, 60, 61
Philip III, king of Spain, 62
Philip V, king of Spain, 66, 69, 72
  arms, 67
Philip, the Handsome, duke of Burgundy, 32–3, 35
*La piazza universale*, 15
Piernas, Pedro, lieutenant-governor of Upper Louisiana, 81
Pinar de la Vidriera (Granada), 53
Plandiura collection, Barcelona, 9
plate glass, 51, 72, 73–5, 77, 80
Poblet, Monastery of, 20, 23, 28
polishing machines, 72, 73–5
Pomeraye, Jean-Baptiste de la, 66
*porró*, 44, 47–8, 49, 51, 56

Portugal, arms, 33, 59
Prague, Umělecko-Průmyslové Museum (Museum of Industrial Art), 10
Prats, Juan, collection, 9, 39
Prats de Molló (Roussillon), 44
Priego, marquis of, 33
prunts, 40, 43
Puebla de Don Fadrique (Granada), 53
Puebla de los Angeles (Mexico), 58

Ramos, Félix, 85
Real Fábrica de Cristales *see* San Ildefonso (Segovia)
Real Sociedad Aragonesa de Amigos del País, 48
Recuenco (Guadalajara), 67–71
  Dorado factory, 69–71
  López de Aragón factory, 69
Riaño collection, London, 52, 83
Riaño y Montero, Bonifacio, 52
Riaño y Montero, Juan, 52
Rico y Sinobas collection, Madrid, 9
Ripoll, Bible of, 19, 72
Roda, Bible of, 19
Rodríguez, Juan, 57–8, 61
Romero y Ortiz, Manuel, 53
Royal Glass Factory *see* San Ildefonso (Segovia)
Ruiz de Castejón, Francisca, 33
Ruiz Dorado *see* Recuenco. Dorado factory

Saint-Gobain, 66
Saint Louis (Missouri), The Missouri Historical Society, 80–1
Salinas (Alicante), 47
San Benet de Bages, Monastery of, 28
San Feliú de Guixols (Gerona), 23
San Ildefonso (Segovia), 79
  Palace of La Granja, 72, 85
  Royal Glass Factory (Real Fábrica de Cristales), 17, 47, 48, 51, 56, 59, 72–87
San Martín de Valdeiglesias (Madrid), 61, 64
Santas Creus, Monastery of, 28
San Vicente dels Horts (Barcelona), 45
Segovia, 64
Seigne, Claude, 77
*setrill*, 38, 49
Sevilla, 57–9
Sicily-Naples, arms, 75
Sit, Ventura, 51, 72, 77
Sivert, Denis, 77
soda-lime glass, 11, 15, 78
Spain, arms, 59
Strauss, Jerome, 9
Suárez, Miguel Jerónimo. Translation of Neri, 82–3
Suárez de Figueroa, Cristóbal, 15

Syrian glass, 22–3, 27, 54

Tarragona, 20, 25
Theophilus. Treatise on glass, 13
Toledo, Hospital of San Juan Bautista, pharmacy, 70
tools for glassmaking, 16, 64
Toreata, Guglielmo, 62–3
Torre de Esteban Hambrán (Toledo), 63
Tortosa (Tarragona), 15, 23, 25, 67
Triguero Serrano factory *see* María (Almería)
Turkey, Sultan of, 76

Utrillas (Teruel), 48

Valdemaqueda (Madrid), 63, 68
Valdepeñas (Jaén), 53
Valencia, 15, 33, 46–8, 51, 59
  Fontvila factory, 47, 51
  glass furnaces, 25, 46
  Virgin of Desamparados, 47
Valladolid, 62
Vallbona (Barcelona), 25, 44
  Can Flor, 44
Valle de Canet collection, 9
Vallromanas (Barcelona), 24
Vallvidrera (Barcelona), 24
Van Halen, Francisco, 73
Veiga, Thomé Pinheiro da, 62
Venetian glasses, 26, 29, 30, 33–5, 39–41, 44, 47, 54, 57, 60–1, 68
Venetian-style glasses, 11–12, 14–15, 28–49, 55–9, 60–9
Venice *see* Murano; Venetian glasses
Vera Cruz (Mexico), 80
Vich, 24, 28, 36, 44
  Museo Episcopal, 44
Victoria and Albert Museum, 10, 36–7, 41, 52, 54, 55, 83
Vidreras (Gerona), 24
Villafranca del Panadés (Barcelona), 28, 50, 51
Villalonga (Roussillon), 25
Villanueva de Alcorón (Guadalajara), 67, 68
Villena factories *see* Cadalso
Vindel (Cuenca), 68, 71
Visigothic glass, 12–13
Vistabella (Zaragoza), 48

wheel-engraving, 11, 66, 67, 72, 77 ff., 82, 85
window-panes, 17, 47, 50, 61, 62, 63, 66, 70, 72

zaffre, 15, 74
Zafra, arms, 53
Zaragoza, 51

1. *Cruet, of transparent greenish glass. From a tomb in the Monastery of San Benet de Bages. Cataluña, fifteenth century. Ht. 4¼ in. (10·8 cm.) Present location unknown; formerly in the collection of Juan Prats Tomás, Barcelona*
(*See pages 28, 49*)

2A. *Wineglass, of uncoloured glass. From a tomb in the cemetery of the Monastery of Santas Creus (Tarragona). Cataluña, late fifteenth century. Ht. 7⅛ in. (18 cm.)*
*Museo Arqueológico Provincial, Tarragona*
*(See page 28)*

2B. *Wineglass, of transparent greyish glass; enamelled, with traces of cold-gilt; trailed cords pincered into a net pattern. Barcelona, about 1500. Ht. 5½ in. (14 cm.) Museos de Arte, Barcelona. Cabot Bequest (See page 28)*

3. *Goblet, of transparent cobalt-blue glass; enamelled and cold-gilt. Barcelona, about* 1500. *Ht.* 8 *in.* (20·3 *cm.*) *The Hispanic Society of America, New York* (*See pages* 28–29, 43)

4. *Vase, of transparent uncoloured glass, with enamelled decorations.*
*Barcelona, sixteenth century. Ht.* 10¾ *in.* (27·3 *cm.*)
*Victoria and Albert Museum*
(*See pages* 37–38, 39)

5A–B. *Serving dish, of transparent uncoloured glass,*
*with enamelled decorations. Barcelona, sixteenth century.*
*Diam. 8⅛ in. (20·6 cm.) Victoria and Albert Museum*
*(See page 38)*

6. *Ewer, of transparent uncoloured glass, with enamelled and cold-gilt decorations. Barcelona, sixteenth century. Ht.* 10⅜ *in.* (26·5 *cm.*)
*Musée de Cluny, Paris*
(*See page* 38)

7A. *Serving dish, of transparent uncoloured glass, with enamelled decorations.*
*Barcelona, sixteenth century. Diam.* $8\frac{1}{4}$ *in.* (21 *cm.*)
*Instituto de Valencia de Don Juan, Madrid* (*See page* 39)

7B. *Aspersory, of transparent uncoloured glass, with enamelled decorations;*
*grooved bail-handle. Barcelona, sixteenth century. Diam.* $5\frac{1}{8}$ *in.* (13 *cm.*)
*Museos de Arte, Barcelona. Cabot Bequest* (*See pages* 38–39)

8. *Covered jar, of transparent uncoloured glass, with enamelled decorations.*
*Barcelona, sixteenth century. Ht.* 9¾ *in.* (24·7 *cm.*)
*Musée de Cluny, Paris*
*(See page* 38)

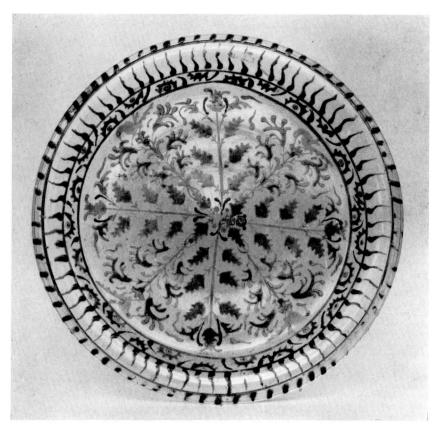

9A. *Sanctuary lamp, of transparent uncoloured glass,*
*with enamelled decorations. Barcelona, sixteenth century.*
*Ht. 3⅛ in. (8 cm.) Museo Episcopal, Vich*
*(See page 39)*

9B. *Plate, of transparent uncoloured glass, with enamelled decorations.*
*Barcelona, sixteenth century. Diam. 7¼ in. (18·4 cm.)*
*British Museum*
*(See page 37)*

10. *Jug, of pale straw-coloured glass, frosted; tooled handle.*
*Cataluña, late sixteenth or early seventeenth century.*
*Ht. 7½ in. (19 cm.) Victoria and Albert Museum.*
*(See page 40)*

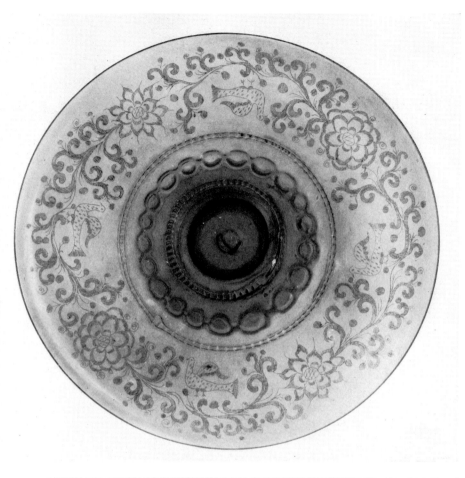

11A–B. *Serving dish, of transparent uncoloured glass,*
*with diamond-point engraving; cobalt-blue trailed threads.*
*Cataluña, early seventeenth century. Diam.* 12¾ *in.* (31·5 *cm.*)
*Museos de Arte, Barcelona. Plandiura Collection*
(*See page* 40)

12. *Wineglass, of transparent uncoloured glass, with trailed opaque white cords; gilt prunts and pincered decoration.*
*Cataluña, sixteenth century. Ht. 5⅞ in. (15 cm.)*
*Miguel Mateu Pla, Peralada*
*(See pages 31, 40–41, 42, 43)*

13. *Wineglass, of transparent yellowish glass, with trailed opaque white cords; hollow lion's-head stem. Cataluña, sixteenth century. Ht. 6 in.* (15·2 cm.)
*Countess of El Valle de Canet, Barcelona*
(*See pages* 40, 42–43)

14A. *Hat, of transparent uncoloured glass, with trailed opaque white cords and blue trimming. Cataluña, c. 1585–95. Ht. 3⅛ in. (8 cm.)*
*Countess of El Valle de Canet, Barcelona*
*(See pages 40–41, 43)*

14B. *Vessel, of transparent uncoloured glass, with trailed opaque white cords. Cataluña, sixteenth century. Museos de Arte, Barcelona*
*(See pages 40–41)*

15A. *Sanctuary lamp, of transparent yellowish glass, with trailed opaque white cords and moulded prunts. Cataluña, sixteenth century. Ht.* $3\frac{1}{8}$ *in. (8 cm.)*
*Miguel Mateu Pla, Peralada*
(*See pages 40–41*)

15B. *Jewel-box, in the shape of a sabot; opaque white stripes, pincered decoration. Cataluña, sixteenth century. Ht.* $3\frac{1}{8}$ *in. (8 cm.)*
*Museo Episcopal, Vich*
(*See page 43*)

16. *Almorratxa, vessel for sprinkling rose-water, of transparent uncoloured glass, with trailed opaque white cords and gilt prunts; pincered net pattern round the rim. Barcelona, late sixteenth century. Ht.* 10¼ *in.* (26 *cm.*)
*Miguel Mateu Pla, Peralada*
(*See pages* 31, 40–41, 49)

17. *Covered jar, of transparent yellowish glass, with trailed opaque white cords
and a pair of gilt bands. Barcelona, late sixteenth century. From a monastery in
Castilla la Vieja. Ht. 18¾ in. (47·5 cm.)
Instituto Amatller de Arte Hispánico, Barcelona
(See pages 38, 40)*

18. *Wineglass, of transparent uncoloured glass, with opaque white stripes;*
*pincered handles and prunts of uncoloured glass. Barcelona, sixteenth century.*
*Ht. 3½ in. (9 cm.) Instituto Amatller de Arte Hispánico, Barcelona.*
*Gift of Juan Prats Tomás, 1962*
(*See pages* 42, 43)

19. *Cup, of transparent yellowish glass, with opaque white stripes; pincered handles; cover missing. Barcelona, late sixteenth century. Ht. 5¼ in. (13·3 cm.)*
*Miguel Mateu Pla, Peralada*

(*See page 42*)

20. *Wineglass, of transparent uncoloured glass, with opaque white stripes spirally twisted; pincered handles and prunts of uncoloured glass. Barcelona, sixteenth century. Ht.* 5½ *in.* (14 cm.) *Museos de Arte, Barcelona. Cabot Bequest* (*See pages* 41, 42)

21. *Wineglass, of transparent uncoloured glass, with opaque white stripes spirally twisted. Cataluña, probably Barcelona, late sixteenth century.*
*Ht.* 5$\frac{3}{16}$ *in.* (14·5 *cm.*)
*Instituto de Valencia de Don Juan, Madrid*
(*See pages* 41, 43)

22. *Cock, of transparent uncoloured glass, with opaque white stripes and cobalt-blue crestings. Cataluña, probably Barcelona, sixteenth century. Ht.* 11¼ *in.* (28·5 *cm.*) *Instituto Amatller de Arte Hispánico, Barcelona.*
Gift of Juan Prats Tomás, 1962
(*See page* 43)

23A. *Cruet, of transparent yellowish glass, with combed opaque white stripes.*
*Cataluña, probably Barcelona, late sixteenth century. Ht. 7½ in. (19 cm.)*
*Musée de Cluny, Paris. (See page 41)*
23B. *Brandy keg, of ultramarine-blue glass, with combed opaque white stripes;*
*trailed and pincered cords. Cataluña, eighteenth century. Length 5⅞ in. (15 cm.)*
*Museo Cau Ferrat, Sitges. (See page 41)*

24. *Decanter, of transparent greyish glass, mould-blown.*
*Barcelona, sixteenth century. Ht. 13 in. (33 cm.)*
*Museos de Arte, Barcelona. Cabot Bequest*
(See pages 40, 42)

25A. *Bowl, of transparent uncoloured glass, blown in a ribbed mould;*
*pincered handles. Cataluña, seventeenth century. Diam.* $5\frac{3}{16}$ *in.* (14·5 *cm.*)
*Instituto de Valencia de Don Juan, Madrid*
(*See page 42*)
25B. *Cup, of transparent glass blown in a pattern mould.*
*Cataluña, eighteenth century. Ht.* $3\frac{1}{8}$ *in.* (8 *cm.*)
*Museo Episcopal, Vich*
(*See page 42*)

26. *Cruet, of pale olive-green glass, blown in a ribbed mould; two handles with pincered decoration. Cataluña, seventeenth century. Ht.* $6\frac{11}{16}$ *in.* (17 cm.) *Museos de Arte, Barcelona. Cabot Bequest*

(*See page* 42)

27A. *Bowl, of transparent yellowish glass; tooled indentations.*
*Cataluña, seventeenth century. Ht. 3⅜ in. (8·5 cm.)*
*Museos de Arte, Barcelona. Cabot Bequest*
*(See page 42)*
27B. *Wineglass, of transparent greenish glass, with pincered opaque white*
*decorations; twisted bowl, pattern-moulded knop.*
*Cataluña, eighteenth century. Ht. 4⅜ in. (11·1 cm.)*
*The Corning Museum of Glass, Corning (New York)*
*(See page 49)*

28. *Two wineglasses, of transparent yellowish glass; (a) mould-blown bowl with widely spaced diamonds; hollow baluster stem; (b) hollow lion's-head stem. Cataluña, sixteenth century. Hts. 5⅝ in. and 6¼ in. (14·3 cm. and 16 cm.) Ruth Bryan Strauss Memorial Foundation and Jerome Strauss, State College (Pennsylvania)*

29. *Two wineglasses, of transparent yellowish glass, hollow stems.*
*Cataluña, seventeenth century. Hts. 5⅜ in. and 5 9/16 in. (13·7 cm. and 14·2 cm.)*
*Jerome Strauss, State College (Pennsylvania)*
*(See pages 42, 43)*

30. *Bucket, of transparent yellowish glass, with trailed thread decoration;*
*blown in a ribbed mould; twisted bail-handle.*
*Cataluña, probably seventeenth century. Ht. without handle* $5\frac{7}{8}$ *in. (15 cm.)*
*Museos de Arte, Barcelona. Cabot Bequest*
*(See page 42)*

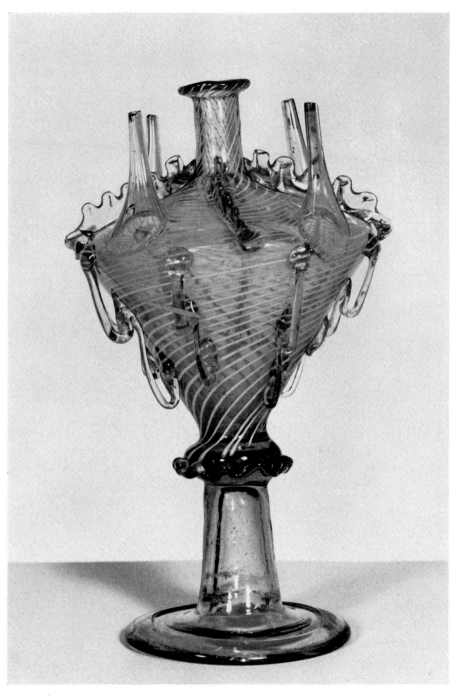

31. *Almorratxa, of transparent uncoloured glass, with opaque white stripes,*
*spirally twisted. Cataluña, eighteenth century. Ht. 9$\frac{1}{8}$ in. (23·2 cm.)*
*The Hispanic Society of America, New York. Acquired in 1961*
*(See page 49)*

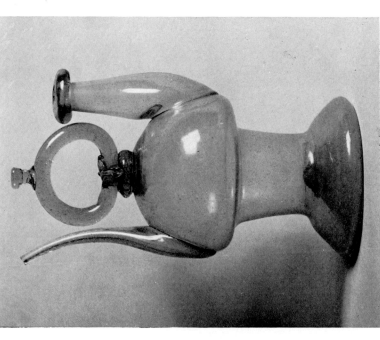

32B. *Càntir, of transparent uncoloured glass.*
*Southern France, eighteenth century. Ht. 7¼ in. (18·5 cm.)*
*The Toledo Museum of Art, Toledo (Ohio).*
*Gift of Edward Drummond Libbey*
(See page 49)

32A. *Water jug, of transparent smoky-grey glass,*
*pincered handles and decoration.*
*Southern France, late seventeenth century. Ht. 7 in. (17·8 cm.)*
*The Toledo Museum of Art, Toledo (Ohio).*
*Gift of Edward Drummond Libbey*
(See page 49)

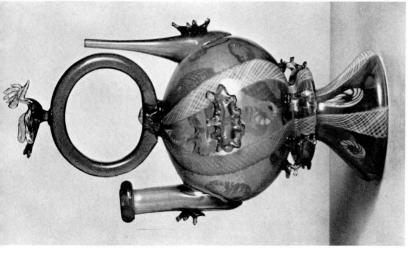

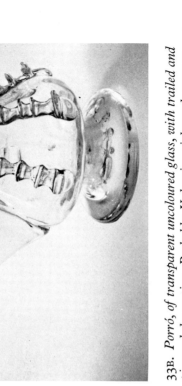

33A. Càntir, of transparent greyish glass, with braided opaque white stripes and pincered decorations. Cataluña, eighteenth century. Ht. 10⅜ in. (26·4 cm.) The Hispanic Society of America, New York (See pages 41, 49)

33B. Porró, of transparent uncoloured glass, with trailed and pincered decoration. Probably Valencia, eighteenth century. Ht. 7¼ in. (18·5 cm.) Jerome Strauss, State College (Pennsylvania) (See pages 47–48)

34. *Porró, of transparent uncoloured glass, with rings and stripes of opaque white in a twisted braid. Cataluña, eighteenth century. Ht.* 8¼ *in.* (21 *cm.*)
*Kunstgewerbemuseum, Berlin*
(*See pages* 41, 49)

35. *Porró, of transparent uncoloured glass, with opaque white stripes.*
*Cataluña, seventeenth–early eighteenth century. Ht.* $9\frac{1}{16}$ *in.* (23 *cm.*)
*Umělecko-Průmyslové Museum, Prague.*
(*See page* 49)

36A. *Oil lamp, with multiple burners. Cataluña, eighteenth century. Ht.* $4\frac{5}{16}$ *in.* (11 *cm.*) *Museo Arqueológico Nacional, Madrid* (*See page* 50)

36B. *Oil lamp, of transparent glass with opaque white stripes, spirally twisted. Cataluña, eighteenth–nineteenth century. Ht.* $7\frac{1}{2}$ *in.* (19 *cm.*) *Museo Arqueológico Nacional, Madrid* (*See pages* 50, 56)

37. *Oil lamp, of marbled glass, with opaque white burners and pincered decoration. Probably Cataluña, eighteenth century. Ht.* 11½ *in.* (20·2 *cm.*)
*Glasgow Art Gallery and Museum*
(*See pages* 50, 56)

38A. *Mug, of transparent glass blown in a pattern mould.
Probably Cataluña, late eighteenth century. Ht.* 5⅛ *in.* (13 *cm.*)
*Museo Episcopal, Vich*
(*See page* 49)

38B. *Mug, of transparent uncoloured glass, with combed opaque
white stripes. Probably Cataluña, late eighteenth century. Ht.*
5⅞ *in.* (15 *cm.*) *Instituto de Valencia de Don Juan, Madrid*
(*See page* 49)

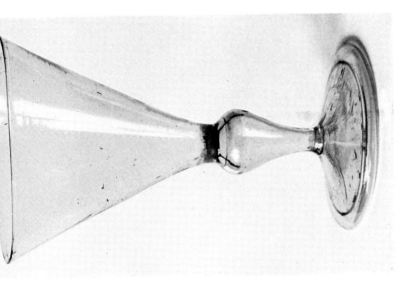

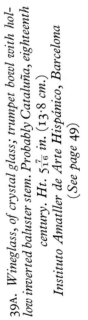

39A. *Wineglass, of crystal glass; trumpet bowl with hollow inverted baluster stem. Probably Cataluña, eighteenth century. Ht. $5\frac{7}{16}$ in. (13·8 cm.)*
*Instituto Amatller de Arte Hispánico, Barcelona*
*(See page 49)*

39B. *Goblet, of transparent uncoloured glass, blown in a pattern mould. Probably Cataluña, eighteenth century. Ht. $6\frac{1}{4}$ in. (15·8 cm.)*
*Umělecko-Průmyslové Museum, Prague*
*(See page 49)*

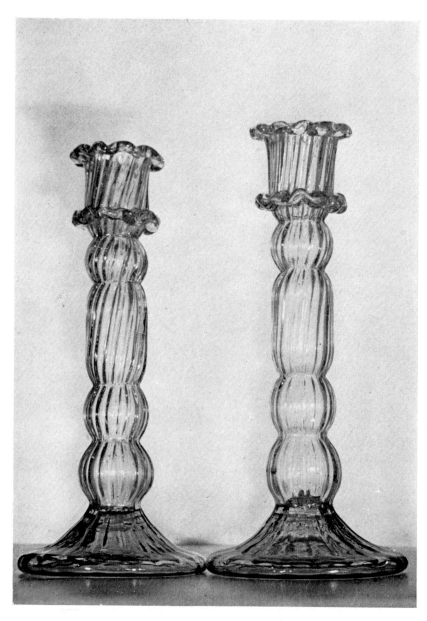

40. *Candlesticks, of transparent greyish glass.*
*Mataró (Barcelona), nineteenth century. Hts. between 7 and 8 in.*
*Glasgow Art Gallery and Museum*
*(See page 50)*

41. *Vase, of transparent glass, with decoration of pincered crestings.*
*Cataluña, eighteenth century. Ht.* $5\frac{7}{8}$ *in.* (15 *cm.*)
*Museo Episcopal, Vich*
(*See page* 50)

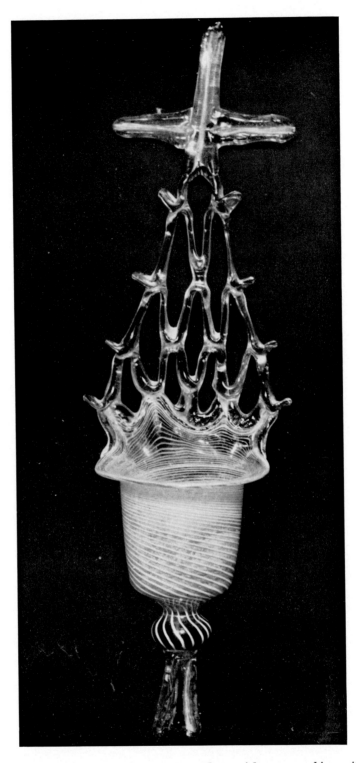

42. *Holy-water stoup, of transparent glass, with opaque white stripes.*
*Cataluña, eighteenth century. Private collection, Barcelona*
(*See page* 50)

43. *Basket, built up with cords of transparent uncoloured glass, pincered decoration. Cataluña, early nineteenth century. Ht.* 8¼ *in.* (21 cm.)
*Macaya collection, Barcelona*
(*See page* 50)

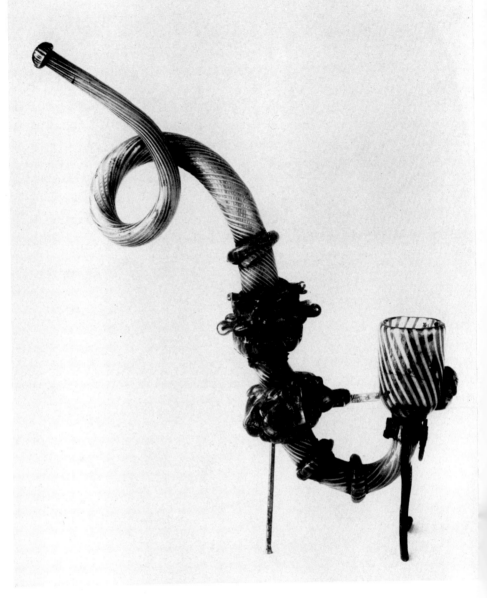

44. *Pipe, of transparent greyish glass, with opaque white stripes; pincered
decoration. Cataluña, eighteenth century. Length 7¼ in. (18·5 cm.)*
*Museos de Arte, Barcelona*
*(See page 50)*

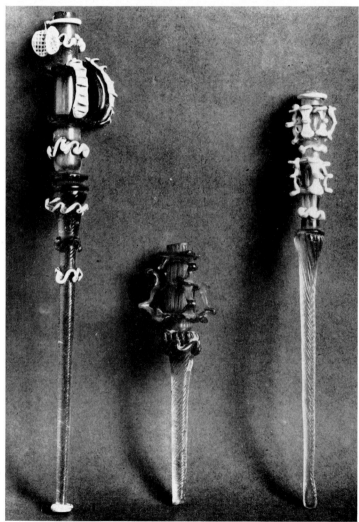

45A. *Lizard, of transparent glass.*
*Cataluña, eighteenth–early nineteenth century. Length* $11\frac{1}{4}$ *in.* (28·5 *cm.*)
*Present owner unknown (See page* 50)
45B. *Spindles. Cataluña, eighteenth–early nineteenth century.*
*Lengths* $9\frac{13}{16}$ *in.,* $6\frac{1}{4}$ *in. and* $11\frac{3}{4}$ *in.* (25 *cm.,* 16 *cm.,* 30 *cm.*)
*Museo Episcopal, Vich (See page* 50)

46. *Vase, of transparent green glass, with threading and pincered decoration;*
*eight tubular handles. Probably Almería province, sixteenth century.*
*Ht. 7¾ in. (19·7 cm.) Victoria and Albert Museum*
*(See page 54)*

47. *Vase, of transparent smoky yellow glass, with threading and pincered decoration. Probably Granada province, seventeenth century. Ht. 7 in. (17·8 cm.)*
*Victoria and Albert Museum*
*(See pages 54, 57)*

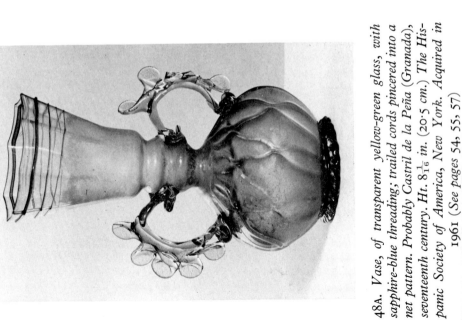

48A. *Vase, of transparent yellow-green glass, with sapphire-blue threading; trailed cords pincered into a net pattern. Probably Castril de la Peña (Granada), seventeenth century. Ht. 8 1/16 in. (20.5 cm.) The Hispanic Society of America, New York. Acquired in 1961 (See pages 54, 55, 57)*

48B. *Vase, of transparent bluish glass, with trailed chain decoration; double tubular handles. Probably Granada province, seventeenth century. Ht. 7 1/2 in. (19 cm.) Instituto de Valencia de Don Juan, Madrid*

(*See pages 54, 57*)

49A. *Jug, of transparent green glass, with threading, trailed chain pattern and pincered decoration. Almería province, seventeenth century. Ht. 7½ in. (19 cm.)* Kunstgewerbemuseum, Cologne

(*See pages 55–56*)

49B. *Jug, of transparent, pale green glass, blown in a ribbed mould; cobalt-blue rim and threading. Granada province, eighteenth century. Ht. 6⅛ in. (15·5 cm.) The Metropolitan Museum of Art, New York. Gift of Henry G. Marquand, 1883*

(*See pages 55–56*)

50. *Goblet-vase, of transparent greenish glass, with trailed chain decoration.*
*Castril de la Peña, seventeenth century. Ht.* 8¼ *in.* (21 *cm.*)
*Museo Arqueológico Provincial, Granada*
(*See page* 55)

51A. *Wineglass, of transparent greenish-yellow glass, with pincered decorations*
*enclosing the hollow stem.*
*Probably Castril de la Peña, early seventeenth century. Ht.* 5½ *in.* (14 *cm.*)
*Ruth Bryan Strauss Memorial Foundation, State College (Pennsylvania)*
*(See page 55)*
51B. *Two bottles, of transparent greenish-yellow and olive-green glasses, with*
*pincered decorations. Granada province, seventeenth–early eighteenth century.*
*Hts.* 6½ *in. and* 5¾ *in.* (16·5 *cm. and* 14·6 *cm.*) *British Museum*
*(See page 55)*

52. *Double cruet, of green glass, with internal partition; trailed threading and pincered cresting on single handle. Spanish, probably Granada province, eighteenth century. Ht.* 6⅝ *in.* (16·8 *cm.*)
*Victoria and Albert Museum*
*(See page* 56)

53A. *Salt dish and bottle, (a) of transparent greenish glass, trimmed with blue;*
*(b) of transparent yellowish-green glass, pincered decorations.*
*Granada province, eighteenth century. Hts. 3 in. and 4 in. (7·6 cm. and 10·1 cm.)*
*Glasgow Art Gallery and Museum*
*(See pages 55, 56)*

53B. *Ornaments, representing doves, of transparent green glass. Granada or*
*Almería province, eighteenth century. Hts. 4½ in. and 4 in. (11·5 cm. and*
*10·1 cm.) Glasgow Art Gallery and Museum*
*(See pages 56–57)*

54. *Oil lamp, of transparent blue-green glass. Granada province, seventeenth–
early eighteenth century. Ht.* 5⅛ *in.* (13 *cm.) Victoria and Albert Museum*
(*See page* 56)

55. *Vase, of transparent green glass, with threading and pincered decorations.*
*Granada province, eighteenth century. Ht. 6¾ in. (17·1 cm.)*
*Victoria and Albert Museum*
*(See page 56)*

56. *Botijo, of transparent yellow-green glass, with threading, trailed chain and pincered decorations. Granada province, seventeenth century. Ht. 8¼ in. (21 cm.)*
*Victoria and Albert Museum*
(*See pages* 56, 57)

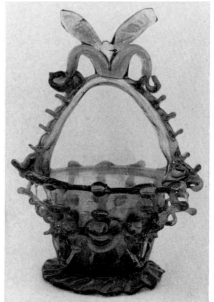

57A. *Cup, of transparent green glass, with pincered decorations. Granada province, eighteenth century. Ht.* 2½ *in.* (6·5 *cm.*)
*Umělecko-Průmyslové Museum, Prague*
(*See page 55*)

57B. *Linen smoother, of green glass. Granada province, eighteenth century. Ht.* 5 5/16 *in.* (13·5 *cm.*) *Museo Arqueológico Nacional, Madrid*
(*See page 56*)

57C. *Bucket, of transparent yellow-green glass, with an elongated bulb of blue-green inside; trailed threading, twisted bail-handle. Ht.* 3½ *in.* (9 *cm.*)
*British Museum*
(*See page 56*)

57D. *Basket, of emerald-green glass, with pincered decorations. Probably María (Almería), eighteenth century. Ht.* 7 5/8 *in.* (19·4 *cm.*)
*The Metropolitan Museum of Art, New York.*
*Bequest of Edward C. Moore, 1891*
(*See page 56*)

58. *Mug, of transparent green glass, overlaid with dark brown.*
*Probably from Almería province, eighteenth century.*
*Ht. 7$\frac{1}{16}$ in. (18 cm.) Kunstgewerbemuseum, Berlin*
*(See pages 54, 55)*

59. *Vase, of transparent blue-green glass overlaid with dark brown; brown handles and threading. Granada province, seventeenth–early eighteenth century. Ht. 5⅝ in. (14·7 cm.) Victoria and Albert Museum*
(*See page* 57)

60. *Vase, of green glass, with four tubular handles hung with rings; threading, trailed chain and pincered decorations. Probably María (Almería), seventeenth century. Ht.* $8\frac{1}{16}$ *in.* (20·5 *cm.*) *Museo Vetrario di Murano, Venice*
(*See page* 54)

61. *Vase, of transparent green glass, with dark brown threading, pincered cresting and rings on multiple handles. María (Almería), seventeenth century. Ht. 9⅞ in. (25 cm.) Kunstgewerbemuseum, Berlin*
(*See pages 54, 57*)

62. *Vase, of blue-green glass, with trailed threading and pincered decoration.*
*Probably María (Almería), seventeenth century. Ht.* 6½ *in.* (16·5 *cm.*)
*British Museum*
(*See page* 54)

63. *Jug, of dark grey-green glass, with combed threading, prunts and pincered cresting on a tubular handle. Probably María (Almería), seventeenth century. Ht. 6¾ in. (17·1 cm.) Victoria and Albert Museum*
(*See page 55*)

64A. *Vase and bottle, of transparent emerald-green glass with*
*pincered decorations. Probably María (Almería), eighteenth century.*
*Hts. 5 in. and 4 in. (12·7 cm. and 10·1 cm.)*
*Glasgow Art Gallery and Museum*
*(See page 55)*

64B. *Pocket glass, of transparent emerald-green, with trailed threading and*
*chain decorations. María (Almería), early seventeenth century.*
*Ht. 4 in. (10·2 cm.) Jerome Strauss, State College (Pennsylvania)*
*(See page 55)*

64C. *Pocket glass, of transparent bluish glass mould blown; inscribed AVE*
*MARIA. María (Almería), early seventeenth century.*
*Ht. 3¾ in. (9·5 cm.) Instituto de Valencia de Don Juan, Madrid*
*(See page 55)*

65A. *Cup, of transparent yellowish glass, with pincered cresting on the tubular
handle and trailed chain decoration. Probably Cadalso de les Vidrios, late
sixteenth or early seventeenth century. Ht.* 5⅛ *in.* (13 *cm.*)
The Hispanic Society of America, New York
(*See page* 65)

65B. *Bowl, of transparent uncoloured glass, with combed opaque white stripes,
pincered handles and rim of blue glass. Probably Cadalso de los Vidrios, late
sixteenth or early seventeenth century. Diam.* 4 5/16 *in.* (11 *cm.*)
Instituto de Valencia de Don Juan, Madrid
(*See page* 65)

66. *Vase, of transparent greenish glass, with opaque white stripes and cobalt-blue rim. Probably Cadalso de los Vidrios, late sixteenth or early seventeenth century. Ht. 5⅛ in. (13 cm.)*
*Museos de Arte, Barcelona. Cabot Bequest*
*(See page 65)*

67. *Goblet, of transparent greenish glass with opaque white stripes; blown from a single gather and twisted; pincered handles and trailed cords of cobalt-blue glass. Probably Cadalso de los Vidrios, late sixteenth or early seventeenth century. Ht.* 6$\frac{5}{16}$ *in.* (16 *cm.*) *Museos de Arte, Barcelona. Cabot Bequest* (*See page* 65)

68. *Vase, of yellowish glass, blown in a pattern mould; stripes of braided opaque white; pincered handles. Castilian, probably Cadalso de los Vidrios, seventeenth century. Ht.* 5⅞ *in.* (15 *cm.*) *Museos de Arte, Barcelona. Cabot Bequest*
(*See pages* 65–66)

69. *Vase, of bubbly greenish glass, with opaque white threading, pincered cobalt-blue cresting on the handles, stripes of purplish brown and opaque white, tooled into scrolls. Cadalso de los Vidrios, seventeenth century.*
*Ht. 4⅞ in. (12·5 cm.) Macaya collection, Barcelona*
*(See page 66)*

70. *Vase, of uncoloured glass, with diagonal ribbing.*
*Probably Recuenco, eighteenth century. Ht. 7⅞ in. (20 cm.)*
*Macaya collection, Barcelona*
*(See page 68)*

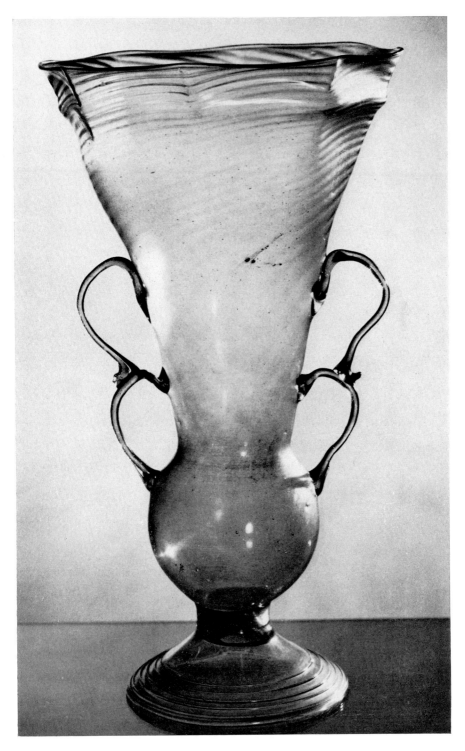

71. *Vase, of greenish glass, with diagonal ribbing.*
*Probably Recuenco, eighteenth century. Ht.* $8\frac{7}{8}$ *in.* (22·5 *cm.*)
*Victoria and Albert Museum*
(*See page* 69)

72. *Goblet-vase, of bubbly green glass, with diagonal ribbing, pincered cresting on the handles. Castillian, probably Recuenco, late seventeenth century. Ht. 9⅛ in. (23·2 cm.) Jerome Strauss, State College (Pennsylvania)*
(*See page* 69)

73. *Vase, of bubbly greenish glass. Castillian, probably Cadalso de los Vidrios,*
*seventeenth century. Ht.* 6⅝ *in.* (16·8 *cm.*)
*Umĕlecko-Průmyslové Museum, Prague*
(*See page* 65)

74. *Vase, of green glass streaked with brown; diagonal ribbing.
Probably Recuenco, eighteenth century. Ht.* $8\frac{1}{16}$ *in.* (20·5 *cm.*)
*Victoria and Albert Museum*
(*See page* 69)

75A. *Vase, of yellowish glass, with sapphire blue handles and threading. Probably Recuenco, eighteenth century. Ht. 5 in. (12·8 cm.) The Hispanic Society of America, New York*
(*See page* 69)

B. *Tumbler, of crystal glass, ~t and engraved with the es-~cheon of Philip V. Nuevo ~ztán (Madrid), about 1725. ~yal Palace, Madrid. (Photo-~ph released and authorized ~y the Patrimonio Nacional)*
(*See page* 67)

76. *Chandelier, of crystal glass, moulded and cut.*
*La Granja de San Ildefonso, late eighteenth century.*
*Antechamber of the Infanta Isabel, Royal Palace, Madrid.*
*(Photograph released and authorized by the Patrimonio Nacional)*
*(See page 76)*

77. *Chandelier, of crystal glass, moulded and cut. La Granja de San Ildefonso,*
*late eighteenth century. Pharmacy of the Royal Palace, Madrid.*
*(Photograph released and authorized by the Patrimonio Nacional)*
*(See page 76)*

78. *Covered jar, of crystal glass, engraved and fire-gilt; faceted knob.*
*La Granja de San Ildefonso, about 1775. Ht. 20 in. (51 cm.)*
*Victoria and Albert Museum*
*(See page 82)*

79. *Decanter, of cut crystal glass. La Granja de San Ildefonso, about* 1775.
*Ht.* 12⅛ *in.* (30·8 *cm.*) *Victoria and Albert Museum*
(*See page* 78)

80. *Three pocket glasses, (a) of transparent blue glass with combed opaque white stripes, (b) of transparent purple glass, with fire-gilt decoration, inscribed 'Dᵃ Vitoriana Baquero', (c) of transparent blue splashed with opaque white. La Granja de San Ildefonso, eighteenth century. Hts. 4⅛ in., 3 3/16 in., 3 3/16 in. (10·5 cm., 8·1 cm., 8·1 cm.) The Corning Museum of Glass, Corning (New York) (See page 83)*

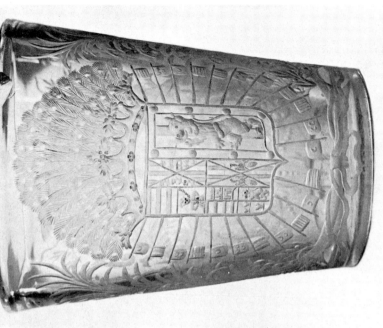

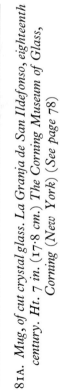

81A. *Mug, of cut crystal glass. La Granja de San Ildefonso, eighteenth century. Ht. 7 in. (17·8 cm.) The Corning Museum of Glass, Corning (New York) (See page 78)*

81B. *Tumbler, of crystal glass, engraved with the escutcheon of the Medinaceli family. La Granja de San Ildefonso, eighteenth century. Ht. 5⅞ in. (15 cm.) Museo Arqueológico Nacional, Madrid (See page 78)*

82. *Decanter, of crystal glass, engraved and fire-gilt.*
*La Granja de San Ildefonso, about* 1775–80.
*Ht.* 12¼ *in.* (31·1 *cm.*) *The Hispanic Society of America, New York*
*(See page 82)*

83. *Decanter of crystal glass blown in a fluted mould and enamelled.*
*La Granja de San Ildefonso, about 1775–85. Ht. 12½ in. (31·8 cm.)*
*Victoria and Albert Museum*
*(See page 84)*

84B. *Mug, of opaque white glass, enamelled. La Granja de San Ildefonso, about 1775–85. Ht. $3\frac{15}{16}$ in. (10 cm.) Museo Arqueológico Nacional, Madrid*
(*See page 84*)

84A. *Mug, of enamelled crystal glass. La Granja de San Ildefonso, about 1775–85. Ht. $5\frac{9}{16}$ in. (14·1 cm.) Ruth Bryan Strauss Memorial Foundation, State College (Pennsylvania)*
(*See page 84*)

85A–B. *Wineglasses, of crystal glass; (a) enamelled, (b) engraved and fire-gilt. La Granja de San Ildefonso, about 1775–85. Hts. 4¾ in. and 4⁵⁄₁₆ in. (12 cm. and 11 cm.) Museo Episcopal, Vich*

(*See pages* 82, 84)

86A. *Tumbler and bottle, of crystal glass, engraved and fire-gilt.*
*La Granja de San Ildefonso, about 1775–85.*
*Hts. 4½ in. and 5 in. (11·5 cm. and 12·7 cm.)*
86B. *Wineglass and salt dish, of crystal glass, engraved and fire-gilt.*
*Hts. 4$\frac{7}{16}$ in. and 1½ in. (11·3 cm. and 3·8 cm.) British Museum*
*(See page 82)*

87. *Tray, of crystal glass, blown in a mould, engraved and fire-gilt.*
*La Granja de San Ildefonso, about 1775–85.*
*Diam. 6¼ in. (15·8 cm.) Victoria and Albert Museum*
*(See page 82)*

88. *Sugar bowl, of crystal glass, engraved and fire-gilt.*
*La Granja de San Ildefonso, about 1775. Ht. 10 in. (25·5 cm.)*
*The Hispanic Society of America, New York*
*(See page 82)*

89A. *Covered bowl, of crystal glass, cut beading and fire-gilt decoration,*
*heraldic charges from the arms of Spain.*
*La Granja de San Ildefonso, eighteenth century.*
*Ht.* 5¼ *in.* (13·3 *cm.*) *Victoria and Albert Museum.* (*See page* 81)
89B. *Sugar bowl, of crystal glass, engraved and fire-gilt.*
*La Granja de San Ildefonso, about* 1785.
*Ht.* 7⅝ *in.* (19·3 *cm.*)
*The Hispanic Society of America, New York.* (*See page* 82)

90B. *Brandy glass of enamelled crystal glass.*
*La Granja de San Ildefonso, about 1775–85.*
*Ht. 3⅛ in. (8 cm.) Hermitage Museum, Leningrad*
(*See page 84*)

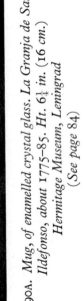

90A. *Mug, of enamelled crystal glass. La Granja de San*
*Ildefonso, about 1775–85. Ht. 6¼ in. (16 cm.)*
*Hermitage Museum, Leningrad*
(*See page 84*)

91. *Glasses from a table service, reputedly owned by Pierre Laclède, founder of Saint Louis, Missouri (d. 1778). Crystal glass, engraved and fire-gilt. La Granja de San Ildefonso, about 1775. The Missouri Historical Society, Saint Louis (See pages 80–81)*

92. *Pharmacy jar, of crystal glass, blown in a mould; with the Spanish royal
arms in enamels and fire-gilt. From the pharmacy of the Royal Palace, Madrid.
La Granja de San Ildefonso, 1794. Ht. 11⅜ in. (29 cm.)
Museo Arqueológico Nacional, Madrid
(See pages 84–85)*

93A. *Bowl, of cut crystal glass; fire-gilt decorations.*
*La Granja de San Ildefonso, early nineteenth century.*
*Ht. 3⅛ in. (8 cm.)*
*The Corning Museum of Glass, Corning (New York)*
*(See page 85)*
93B. *Bowl, of cut crystal glass; fire-gilt decorations.*
*La Granja de San Ildefonso, early nineteenth century.*
*Ht. 3 in. (7·7 cm.)*
*The Corning Museum of Glass, Corning (New York)*
*(See page 85)*

94. *Plaque, of crystal glass, engraved by Félix Ramos. Façade of the Royal Palace of San Ildefonso, facing the gardens. La Granja de San Ildefonso, late eighteenth century.*
*Total ht. 17¹¹⁄₁₆ in. (45 cm.) Ht. of plaque 6¹¹⁄₁₆ in. (17 cm.)*
*W. of plaque 9¹⁄₁₆ in. (23 cm.)*
*Museo Arqueológico Nacional, Madrid*
*(See page 85)*

95. *Table top, of cut crystal glass; painted in oils, perhaps by Vicente López
y Portaña, and mounted in ormolu.
Le Granja de San Ildefonso, 1819–29. Diam. 26 in. (66 cm.)
Royal Palace, Madrid.
(Photograph released and authorized by the Patrimonio Nacional)
(See pages 86–87)*

96. *Covered jar, of enamelled crystal glass, moulded mushroom knob.*
*La Granja de San Ildefonso, about 1775–85.*
*Ht. 8⅝ in. (22 cm.) Museo Arqueológico Nacional, Madrid*
*(See page 84)*